Cress and Marion Reed
Orkney 2006.

WHIT LIKE THE DAY?

understanding Orkney dialect

WHIT LIKE THE DAY?

understanding Orkney dialect

Gregor Lamb

Bellavista Publications

ISBN 0 9550586 0 0

First published in 2005

Published by
Bellavista Publications, 3 Sabiston Crescent, Kirkwall, Orkney, KW15 1YT
Telephone 01856 878196

E-mail Address: bellavistabb@yahoo.co.uk

Printed by Newton Printing Ltd., London

Acknowledgements

I sincerely acknowledge the kindness of the many people who have helped me to produce *Whit Like the Day?* Special thanks go to the publisher, Stewart Davidson who first of all floated the idea of the book. It so happened that I had with me on that day the rough draft of a manuscript which had been started in an interesting way. Over a period of twenty years I had been adapting for radio the celebrated Stenwick stories which had been written by R. T. Johnston in a period spanning the 1930s to the 1960s. These tales were set in an imaginary West Mainland parish and peopled by a host of interesting worthies, all of whom spoke excellent Orkney dialect! All descriptive passages in the stories were written in Standard English but all conversations among Stenwick folk themselves were written in Orkney dialect, a remarkable achievement for Johnston who was a native of Banffshire. These radio adaptations involved not only summarising the stories but also re-writing the Standard English element in dialect to retain flow in the spoken word. It was in the re-writing of this element that I often had to ask myself, 'How would an Orcadian say that?' This led to the formulation of 'rules' for the dialect which form the basis of this book. The simple draft which began this project has gone through many changes since then but retains the idea of analysing our dialect, comparing it with Standard English and Scots and showing that, in the English speaking world, it has many unique features.

I should like to thank Howie Firth, formerly of BBC Radio Orkney, who re-introduced me to the Stenwick stories and who encouraged me greatly to broadcast them. A similar incentive was given to me by John Fergusson the current incumbent at BBC Radio Orkney. The production of the CD would have been impossible without the technical advice and help of John and his opposite number, Steve Haigh of BBC Somerset Sound.

The name Jim Baikie is known throughout the world as a comic strip artist. I have known Jim and his family for many years and I was very pleased to learn that he had undertaken to provide the artwork for the dust jacket and to illustrate the book with cartoons. R. T. Johnston, the author of the Stenwick tales, was also a brilliant cartoonist and contributed many topical cartoons to the local newspaper the *Orkney Herald* in addition to his tales. Jim's contributions add a distinctive Stenwick flavour to the book!

Manuscripts have to be thoroughly checked before they go to press. What better person to ask in this connection than Margaret Flaws whose interest in dialect goes back many, many years. In the early 1980s, long before it became Government policy to foster native speech in schools, an article in the *Times Educational Supplement* at that time revealed that Margaret was making the pupils of Firth School aware of the richness of local dialect. Later it gave me great pleasure to support her in the publication of the *Orkney Dictionary* for use in schools. I am very grateful to Margaret for looking over the manuscript and for making the many suggestions which I have implemented.

Lastly I should like to thank all Orcadians who, unwittingly, have given me so many examples of dialect usage and from whom I have quoted liberally!

Gregor Lamb
26 May 2005

Introduction

If you are an Orcadian and persist to the end of this book you will have done well. For the first time you will have tried to understand the rules of the dialect you speak and they are extremely complex. I am sure that at times you will say to yourself, 'I don't understand that', but as a young child and before the age of five you possessed the remarkable facility to acquire all the rules apparently without actively learning them. Sometimes you made small mistakes like, 'Me goed tae toon wi me granny' but gradually these errors were ironed out and you became completely fluent. On going to school you discovered a new language, English, with new rules, but I doubt if you ever complained to your parents that you could not learn it. It was 'absorbed' just like the local dialect and as a child you learned to switch between one and the other quickly and with ease. An Orkney teacher who spoke dialect in the family regularly walked with her daughter to school. She told me she had noticed that, as soon as her child entered the school gate, 'mammy' became 'Miss' and she immediately began to address her mother in Standard English!

If Orcadians know the rules of their dialect, what is the point of producing a grammar? The object is two-fold. Firstly it will help to show Orcadians that the dialect they speak is not in any way wrong; it has a structure like any other language. Secondly it will help non-Orcadians who have an interest in our dialect to understand it — and maybe even to speak it but the task ahead for non-Orcadians is very much greater than it is for Orcadians since the template for language acquisition peaks in our early years. There are the further problems, common to all languages, in that acquiring a language is not merely acquiring a knowledge of the grammar but also of building vocabulary and gaining familiarity with correct pronunciation and intonation. If you have attempted to learn a foreign language you will have realised that once fluency is acquired, it is most important to live in the environment of the language otherwise the facility to use it soon wanes. Orcadians who have emigrated and who have had little opportunity to meet fellow islanders return home and immediately find that, no matter how hard they try, something of their dialect has been lost. Some regrettably lose it intentionally, believing that it is wrong. Those who deliberately lose their native tongue are said in dialect 'tae spaek proper' or 'tae chant'. Orcadians do not look favourably on those who 'chant' and those who 'chant' badly, confusing dialect and Standard English, are the butt of many jokes! Gerald Meyer, former editor of *The Orcadian* was amused when an Orcadian, in an over friendly gesture, patted him on the back saying 'Gerry, you're a right fine chap!' unfortunately he chanted badly and it came out as 'Cherry you're a right fine Jap'!

In the past the islands have had at least one Director of Education who said that one function of the school was to eradicate dialect. Fortunately in recent years more enlightened people have been at the helm. It is not widely known that one of Orkney's most famous poets had similar sentiments, believing that one function of education was to sweep away dialect. It is a great credit to George Mackay Brown who had national and international recognition, that he not only treasured his dialect but drew heavily on all aspects of island life in his writings.

I hope that this small volume will add to your understanding of the 'mither tongue', that it will add to your appreciation of it and encourage its continued use.

Contents

Dedication

To Lily and Len

for their help

and friendship

What is Grammar?

At school I studied English grammar. I enjoyed it and when it came to learning foreign languages I found it invaluable. In later life it was a revelation to me that the dialect which I spoke also had a grammar. I had thought that I had been brought up to speak bad English! A grammar of the Shetland dialect was published more than fifty years ago and has recently been reprinted. A very simple grammar of the Orkney dialect was included in the *Orkney Dictionary* which was originally published for use in schools but it was felt that a more comprehensive study of the dialect was necessary. The format of this grammar book is very similar to its Shetland counterpart but differs greatly in how usage of the dialect is shown. In the case of the Shetland grammar, all examples are drawn from the writings of Shetlanders; in this book the writer provides all the examples from his own personal experience.

It is hoped that Orcadians and others are not put off by the word 'grammar'. The purpose of grammar is to provide names for the different aspects of a language or a dialect and with these names to provide rules for their use. Before we can make any sense of languages or dialects we do have to give names to the different types of words and how they are used but it is such a pity that the Latin scholars who coined the names for the different parts of speech more than five hundred years ago chose such difficult words and that these words have remained with us ever since. If readers persist in going through this book they will find that these difficult names relate to very simple ideas.

Orkney dialect is seen today as a branch of Scots called

'Insular Scots' and differs considerably in a number of respects from mainland Scots dialects aside from the pronunciation and intonation which are unique. Nevertheless Scots will find much in this book which will be familiar to them. Since languages and dialects are in a constant state of flux, the rules of grammar can relate only to a particular time in their development; all grammar books therefore have a short life-span! Had a grammar of the Orkney dialect been produced in the 1900s, it would need to be extensively revised now. The approach taken in this book to the study of the grammar of Orkney dialect is similar to that adopted in many English grammar books such as Thomson and Martinet's *A Practical English Grammar* published by Oxford University Press. In such texts the grammar of the language is studied from the point of view of parts of speech, beginning with nouns and moving on to more and more difficult aspects. Under each part of speech in this book many dialect examples are given to illustrate usage.

Any study of the grammar of a dialect or language operates under a number of principal constraints. In the case of English there is no such thing as 'Standard English'. It is entirely artificial, having been built up over the years as an approximation of Middle Class English in the Home Counties. It also has to be revised from time to time as fashions change in modes of expression. Similarly there is no such thing as Orkney dialect! There are a number of Orkney dialects but all have something in common which helps the writer to construct, what he believes to be, a useful grammar. Fashions in dialect change too and the reader will find references in the text to what 'older people say'. For this reason many readers, particularly the young and those who have been brought up in Kirkwall or Stromness, can be pardoned if they have never heard of some dialect usages. It emphasises the fact that dialect is in a state of flux but they can be reassured that such usages still exist at the time of writing.

Just as English grammar is based on the language of the Home Counties, this grammar is based on the dialect of the West Mainland of Orkney but reference is made to other areas of Orkney from time to time where significant differences exist. The writer hopes that the West Mainland dialect is reasonably representative of Orkney dialect generally and sincerely welcomes comments on dialect usage from all corners of Orkney.

Nouns

A noun refers to a person, an animal, a thing or an idea. Orcadians use many English nouns, and many Scots nouns but they also use nouns which have their origin in the Old Norse language once spoken in the islands. Listing all such nouns is outside the scope of this book but a representative sample may be found in the Appendix. It is important to point out that some common English nouns are rarely used in dialect. A good example is the word 'woman'. It is used only by a male addressing a female in a familiar way as in *Come on (w)umman!* Orcadian speakers otherwise use the word *wife* as in *Whar wir that wife I saa yi spaekan tae?* 'Bread'* in English usually applies to loaves. In Orkney dialect 'bread' is used only in a specific way applied to the traditional home-baked *bannock* forms such as *floory bread, bere bread* and *oat bread* whereas a loaf of bread is called a *lof.* The noun 'piece' is used as in English but it has a variety of other meanings such as 'sandwich', 'quite a distance', 'place' and 'much'! Here are examples of usage. 'Some children bring a sandwich to school for their dinner,' will be spoken as *Some bairns tak a piece tae the school fur thir dinner.* 'It's quite a distance to walk' will be expressed as *Hid's a piece tae waak.* In dialect, the English sentence, 'There's no place to put a fridge in my kitchen' takes the form *Thir's no piece tae pit a fridge in me keetcheen.* English 'mantelplace' is *mantelpiece* in Orkney dialect. *A piece* is frequently used in the sense 'much' as in *He's a piece better the day* meaning, 'He's much better today'.

The two nouns 'heap' and 'pile' which are used in English to

---

* 'bread' is pronounced 'breed' in the North Isles

describe a mass of material are also used in dialect to describe a large number of people or animals:

'Many people don't like the new ferry time-table' can be expressed as:

A haep o fok don't like the new ferry time-table. *

'There were many cattle at the mart today' can take the form:

Thir wir a haep o baest at the mart the day.

'A big herd of cattle on the road held us up' may be spoken of in this way:

A gret pile o kye on the road held iss ap.

'Pile' may also be used in dialect to describe a quantity of water:

'After that night of rain there was an awful lot of water in that field':

Efter that night o weet thir wir some pile o watter in that field.

Several nouns used in dialect carry a completely different meaning from Standard English and can lead to confusion. A visitor to Orkney who developed a migraine was advised to lie down and put her head on a 'cod'. A *cod* in dialect is a 'pillow'!

The Plural of Nouns

Most words have plural forms where they refer to more than one instance. In the Old Norse language plural forms usually added an 'r' to the word. No Orkney dialect word which has its origin in Norse uses this plural form today but some place-names still show the old Norse form such as Howar, which means 'mounds' or Nouster which describes 'boat shelters'. All nouns today usually add 's' in common with most English words but Orkney dialect, like English, has some irregular plurals. The plural of 'trout' in English is 'trout' but the plural in Orkney

*also 'teeble'

dialect is *troots*. The plural of *lof* is *lof*. 'Give me two loaves' is:
Gae me twa lof.

'Beast' is pronounced *baest*. The plural is also *baest*. The word *baest* is frequently used for 'cow' in dialect but never for other farm animals. I once heard an old lady say:

Me son his no baest, jist sheep, i.e. 'My son has no cattle, only sheep.'

For English 'tooth' and 'foot' Orkney dialect uses the English plural form for both singular and plural!

'I've had one tooth pulled today' is:
Ah'm hin wan teeth tin oot the day.

'I've sprained my foot' is:
Ah'm sprained me feet which seems a nonsense to an English speaker since it would be unusual to sprain both feet at once!

In measuring, Standard English speaks of e.g. 'a man six foot tall' whereas dialect is more logical in its mode of expression, *a man six feet taal.* Dialect is also more logical in describing a 'toothbrush' as a *teethbrush* and 'footprints' as *feetprints*!

The plural of 'horse' is *horse* but the plural of *coo* (English 'cow') is *kye* which is the Old English plural *cȳ*. Where English words are used in dialect in such a way that they describe a number or quantity, some do not take plural form even though they are plural:

'We took three trailer loads of stones out of that field' is:
We tuk three trailer <u>load</u> o stones oot o that field.

'The foundation is forty paces long and twenty wide':
The found is forty pace long and twenty wide.

'I have two pounds of butter in the cupboard'.
I hiv two* pund o butter in the press.

'The peat bank is three peats deep.'
The paet bank is three paet deep.

Contrast the use of the singular/plural forms of 'peat' here with the following example:

---

*also 'twa'

Standard English speaker: 'Do you burn peat?'

Orkney dialect speaker: *Yaas I burn paets.*

A number of Standard English units of time have no plural in dialect if the are preceded by a number or 'many'. Here are examples:

OWER TWENTY 'EAR OWLD

That cat is ower twenty 'ear owld. (Notice that the 'y' of 'year' is not pronounced).

Doreen's in Paris noo; thir sayan she'll be there fur six month.

I waited fur aboot five 'oor and he niver kam.

Contrast these examples which have a number or expression in front of them with these which have no number:

Ah'm no seen him fur 'ears.

Hid'll tak yi months and months tae feeneesh this.

The 'oors I hiv tae wirk is been changed.

Several old plurals were used in Orkney until recently. In the early 1980s a pupil in Stenness Primary School, probably mimicking a grandparent, said to me,'*I canna find* (rhymes with 'wind') *me sheun.*' 'Shoon' is the old English plural of 'shoes' but the vowel has been modified in Orkney dialect. A new English chain of shoe shops has revived the name, choosing SHOON as its brand name! Old folk in Orkney used *een* as the plural of eyes but it is very doubtful if this plural form is heard today. Orcadians shared with Scots the word *owsen* to describe 'oxen'.

Irregular Orkney Dialect Singular Nouns

English Singular	Orkney Dialect Singular
foot	*feet*
tooth	*teeth*

Irregular Orkney Dialect Plurals

Singular	Plural
troot	*troots*
coo	*kye*
horse	*horse*
baest (cow)	*baest*

Several English nouns ending in 'f' or 'fe' drop the termination in their plural forms and add 'ves'. Orkney dialect struggles with such a change, accepting some and rejecting others: 'sheaf' which is pronounced *shaef* becomes *shaeves* and 'leaf' which is pronounced *laef* becomes *laeves*. The plural of 'calf' is regularly *calves*. The following words have irregular plurals:

English Singular	Orkney Dialect Plural
half	*halfs*
knife	*knifes*
life	*lifes*
shelf	*shelfs*
thief	*thiefs*
loaf	*lof*
wife	*weeman*

English plural <u>Pronouns</u> which end in 'ves' are also irregular in dialect: 'ourselves', 'yourselves' and 'themselves' become *wirsels, yirsels* and *themsels/thirsels*.

Three pronouns used in local dialect have unusual plurals:

<u>Singular</u>	<u>Plural</u>
buddy (person)	*fok* (folk)
man-buddy	*men-fok*
wife-buddy	*weeman-fok*

Thir's a buddy coman doon the road. Na feth, thir's three fok.
See the section on Pronouns for a further discussion.

Forms of Address and Commands

The noun 'boy' is of special interest since, when it is used vocatively (i.e. addressing someone) it is pronounced *beuy*. A father might address a badly behaving son with the words:
Come here beuy!
Beuy is also used in an exclamation of surprise on hearing a piece of interesting news as in this conversation:
Speaker: *Me fither's a hunder 'ear owld the day.*
Listener: *Beuy! He's winderfil fur his age.*
Sometimes the exclamation *Beuy for that!* meaning 'Goodness me!' or the plural form of the exclamation — *Beuys! Beuys!* can be heard.
Another interesting noun in this respect is 'man'. It is normally pronounced as in Standard English but when it is used vocatively it is pronounced *min*.
A form of address used by men on meeting is:
Aye, aye min or *Yaas min.*

In an exclamation a common utterance is:

Min fur that! which, like *Beuy fur that!* means 'Goodness me!'

Both *beuy* and *min* are used by males to address other males of any age. A father might order his young son away from a dangerous situation by saying:

Git oot o here min! Similarly an elderly gentlemen on meeting another of similar age might greet him with the words:

Weel beuy, whit like the day?

A very old form of address was formerly used in Birsay. It has been out of use for many years but I have heard the elderly refer to it. Two men on meeting might have exchanged the greeting *Aye gullie!* A similar greeting was recorded in Sanday. This form of address is so old that we have to go back to Gothic to find something similar! In that language the verb *gōljan* was 'to greet'.

The word *buddo,* a term of endearment used in addressing a child or an elderly woman, is still frequently heard. It is not connected in any way with *buddy* meaning 'person' but represents 'bud' (in the sense of 'shoot of a plant') used at one time in the same way in English. In dialect, the diminutive suffix 'o' is attached. In Shakespeare's *King John,* Constance said of her dying son:

> *But now will canker sorrow eat my <u>bud</u>*
> *And chase the native beauty from his cheek.*

Diminutives of Nouns/Names

The old English diminutive 'ock' is still commonly attached to dialect words in Orkney. It is rare in English today being retained in such words as 'bullock' and 'hillock'. In Orkney it has undergone a considerable modification, taking the forms *ick*, *oo* or simply *o* as in the *buddo* form referred to above. *Ick* is used generally in a crescent sweeping from Stromness, through the South Isles and into the East Mainland. *Oo* is used in Birsay, Sandwick and Harray and *o* elsewhere. The 'lapwing' for example is normally called the *teeick*, *teeoo* or *teeo*, depending on which part of Orkney the speaker hails from. In Stromness a young coalfish is called a *piltick*. In Birsay the Devil was, of old, called *Pyoloo*. Personal names such as William are rendered familiarly by Billick, Billoo or Billo.

Articles

Nouns are usually preceded by 'a' or 'the'. These are called 'articles'. The article 'a' or 'an' indicates that we are not talking about any specific object or person. It is therefore called the Indefinite Article. The article 'the', in contrast, relates to a definite object or person and is therefore called the Definite Article:

'Would you like <u>a</u> biscuit?' — i.e. any biscuit, or:

'Would you like <u>the</u> biscuit?' (with the jam centre)

Sometimes nouns do not need articles as for example in the sentence:

'<u>Rain</u> is good for <u>crops</u>' — but this does not concern us in dialect.

Indefinite articles 'a' and 'an'

Unlike English, 'a' is used frequently instead of 'an' in front of nouns or their adjectives beginning with a vowel:

Ah'll boil <u>a</u> egg tae yir tea.

Efter the watter men wir been thir wir jist <u>a</u> explosion o watter fae the tap.

Wir hivan <u>a</u> early tea the night fur wir gan tae the concert in the toon.

An exception to this rule are two words used in dialect to express degree. One of these words is the frequently used adjective *aafil*, i.e. 'awful'.

An aafil lot o fok here the night min.

Sometimes the indefinite article 'an' is prefixed to *aafil* but with the loss of the 'a'.

Naafil lot o fok here the night min.
Sometimes in this example the noun 'lot' is omitted
Naafil o fok here the night min.
Another adjective which behaves in exactly the same way is 'enormous'.
Normous o fok here the night min.

Definite Article 'the'

This article is frequently used in dialect where English would omit it:
I didna go tae <u>the kirk</u> yesterday fur I wirna feelan weel.
I saa the bairns coman home fae <u>the school</u>.
I must go tae <u>the toon</u> and get some nails.
He tuk tae <u>the laugheen</u>.
Occupations such as 'masonry', 'carpentry', 'plumbing' etc., are expressed in dialect as *mason wark, joiner wark, plumbeen wark* and are always preceded by the definite article:
'I worked at carpentry for some time' would be expressed as:
I wirked at the joiner wark a while.
The definite article is very commonly used when talking of time:
I must deu the washeen <u>the day</u>.
The day is used especially in the common greeting, *'Whit like <u>the day</u>?'* which means. 'How are you today?'
I think Ah'll laeve me washeen tae <u>the morn</u> (tomorrow).
The doctor's coman <u>the morn's morneen</u> (tomorrow morning).
Whit are yi deuan <u>the night</u>?
Hid's been a poor summer <u>the year</u>.
In <u>the winter</u> I usually pit me boat in the garage.
He's no been able tae go oot fae <u>the New Year</u>.
In Scots the word 'yestreen' (yester evening) was used to

mean 'last night'. This word was adopted into Orkney dialect but corrupted to _the streen_. It may still be heard in use in the North Isles.

Older people may be heard apostrophising the days of the week as in this example:

I gid ower tae see him on Friday's night.

In contrast 'Neuar Day' (New Year's Day) in dialect is not apostrophised:

Hid's no many thit go aboot on Neuar Day noo — the breathalyser's pitten a stop tae hid.

Adjectives

Adjectives are used to describe a noun or a pronoun. They describe colour, shape, number, feeling etc., but they can also describe ownership in which case they are called possessive adjectives. In the Old Norse language of Orkney adjectives came behind the noun. We can see examples of this in place-names such as *Howan Greeny*, the green mound, or *Bakkan Swarto*, the black slope, but perhaps the best example is Eynhallow, *eyin helga*, the holy island. In the dialect of today adjectives assume the normal English position. Some English adjectives are rarely used in dialect e.g. 'little' even though the English word closely approximates Old Norse where it took the form *lítill*. In the *Orkneyinga Saga* for example Papa Stronsay was referred to as *Papey in Litla* to distinguish it from the bigger, what is now, Papa Westray. There are still many examples of the use of 'little' in Orkney place-names today such as Little Billiafiold in Birsay and Rysa Little in Walls. *Sma/smaal* is commonly used for 'small'. *Smá* was used in Norse times too; the place-name Smoogarth in Firth is 'small farm'. By far the most common dialect word used for 'small' is *peedie* which has largely supplanted *peerie*. The *Peedie Sea* of today in Kirkwall was formerly the *Peerie Sea*. Shetlanders continue to use 'peerie' but in Orkney it is heard only among the older generation. *Peerie* and *peedie* are diminutives of lost dialect words meaning 'small'. The original form of *peerie* can be seen in *pirrens* = *pir anes*, literally 'little ones' and formerly used in the South Isles for 'children'. When the writer was young, the family cat had the name *Peedo,* a name inherited from a generation of cats going back to the 19th century. It shows an original *peed* with the diminutive *o* as a suffix. Scots 'wee' is rarely heard but Scots 'bonny' is regularly used for 'beautiful' though it is pronounced with a more guttural 'o'. The use of 'ill' is shunned, speakers preferring to use *no weel,* i.e. 'not well'. Notice the dialect idiom *tae tak no weel,* 'to become ill'. This practice of expressing something negative in a positive manner can also be seen in the Orcadian use of *no bad* which really means 'quite good'!

It should be noted that the adjective 'annoyed' carries a completely different meaning in Orkney dialect. My sister-in-law spoke to me on the telephone saying:

I wis right annoyed whin yi didna come last night. The sentence suggests that she was very angry. In fact she was very worried about my non-appearance since 'concern' is the meaning carried by 'annoyed' in dialect.

Here are some examples of dialect usage:

'When I was little I had beautiful fair hair' will translate as:

Whin I wir peedie I hid bonny fair hair.

Orkney dialect does not use 'much' on its own as an adjective:

'There's much work to be done yet before we move in' will be spoken in this way:

Thir's a lot o wark tae be done yit afore we mov in.

'So much' is used as in English:

Thir's so much tae deu here afore we mov in.

'Many' on its own is not used positively as an adjective in Orkney dialect. In the example:

'Many people have been asking me if the shop's open tomorrow' becomes:

A lot o fok are been askan me if the shop's open the morn.

Although the adjective 'many' is not used in dialect, the adjectival phrase *many a* is common. The sentence, 'Many would be thankful for that bread you have thrown away', could be expressed as:

Many a buddy wid be thankfil fur that bread yir thrown awey.

The expression *many a day* is frequently used to describe 'a long period of time' as in:

Wir no seen John fur many a day which translates the English sentence:

'We haven't seen John for a long time'.

Many's the day may frequently be heard also describing 'something ongoing for a long period of time', as in:

MANY'S THE DAY AH'M HIN TAE MILK THE COO

Many's the day Ah'm hin tae milk the coo, a rendering of English:

'I often had to milk the cow'.

As in the case of 'much', when 'many' is preceded by 'so', it is used as in Standard English:

So many fok are been askan me if the shop's open the morn.

'Many' is used negatively as an adjective:

'There aren't many cars in the car park today' becomes:

Thir's no many cars* in the car park the day.

Two adjectives which are used in dialect in an interesting way are *grand* and *gret* (great). *Grand* is used in the sense of 'particularly fine'. Here are illustrations of usage:

'It's a really lovely day today'.

Hid's a grand day the day.

---

* In many parts of Orkney 'ar' is pronounced 'er', in which case 'car' is sounded *ker*.

'He's bought a lovely new car'.

He's bowt a grand new car.

Apart from its use meaning 'large', *gret* is also used to mean 'wonderful', 'well' or 'in good shape'. Here are examples of how this word is used:

'It's wonderful that he has been able to come'.

Hid's gret thit he's been able tae come.

'I'm feeling in good shape today'.

Ah'm feelan gret the day.

Gret is more frequently used negatively in the expression *no gret:*

'I have just been to hospital and I'm afraid that Peter isn't very well.'

Ah'm jist been tae the ospital and I doot Peter's no gret.

The adjectival phrase *gret fur* means 'to be fond of':

He's gret fur his fish supper on a Setterday night.

See also the use of *gret* and *grand* under Adverbs.

THIR'S WAAR PIECES TAE BIDE UR STENWICK*

* a fictitious Orkney parish immortalised in the writings of R. T. Johnston

Comparative and Superlative Forms of Adjectives

Examples in English of regular comparative forms of adjectives are 'big', 'bigger', 'biggest' and 'funny', 'funnier', 'funniest'. In these instances 'bigger'; and 'funnier' are said to be the 'comparative' forms of the adjectives. 'Biggest' and 'funniest' are the superlative forms. Some adjectives in English have irregular forms of comparative and superlative. Examples of irregular forms are 'good', 'better', 'best' and 'many', 'more', 'most'. Orkney dialect forms follow English closely with the exception of 'bad', 'worse', 'worst' which is expressed in dialect as:

bad, waar, warst

Notice the dialect idiom *He's gin bae the waar*, 'He has become worse'.

In comparing two objects or ideas English uses the word 'than'.

'Go today — it's better than going tomorrow' reads in dialect as:

Go the day — hid's better than gan the morn.

Orkney dialect speakers sometimes use *ur* (i.e. 'or') instead of 'than' in comparisons:

'Goodness me, that cheese is more than five pounds a pound!' may be expressed as:

Mercy that cheese is more ur five pound a pund! (Notice that Orkney dialect distinguishes between pound (money) and pound (weight).

'He's much better now than he was':

He's a piece better noo ur he wir.

Reference has already been made to the interesting use of adjectives in place-names. *Appie* was formerly used as the comparative form of *ap* (i.e. 'up') in place-names and can be seen in the several Appiehoose/Appieteen place-names in the islands which applied to houses/fields 'higher up'. Houses

subsequently built higher than the 'high' houses were called
uimost houses, i.e. 'upmost' houses! There were houses by this
name in Stronsay. The adjective *nether* was applied to the lower
houses/fields as in Netherhouse/Netherton.

Possessive Adjectives

In English these are 'my', 'your (singular)', 'his', 'her', 'its',
'our', 'your (plural)', 'their'.
Orkney dialect shows the following variations:
me, yir (singular)/*thee, his, har, hids, wir, yir* (plural), *thir**.
The use of 'me' as 'my' in English dialects is very common.
'Give me my hammer' can be expressed in dialect as:
Shaa me me hammer. (*'Shaa'* here is a special use of English
'show' and means 'give' or 'pass').
'Take your time now and don't be working too hard' is:
Tak thee time noo and don't be wirkan too hard+.
'This is our ball so you can't play with it' becomes:
This is wir ball so yi canna play wi hid.
'The cat's lost its collar' is:
The cat's lost hids collar.

Demonstrative Adjectives

In English the Demonstrative Adjectives are 'this' and 'that'.
Both words are used in Orkney dialect. The plural of 'this' is
'these' and the plural of 'that' is 'those'. Such plural forms are
not used in dialect. Only the singular is used. Here are some
examples:
'Have you seen these books?'
Are yi seen this books?
'Those fields are the ones that are to be sold'.
That fields is the wans thit's gan tae be selt.

* *'wur'* and *'yur'* are also heard
+ also pronounced *'herd'*

This use of the singular form of the Demonstrative Adjective produces a tendency to use the singular form of the verb:

This regulations is jist gittan rideeclous (ridiculous).

In the North Isles of Orkney the Demonstrative Pronoun *yin* is used instead of 'that':

'Where's that thing I used the other day?'

Whar's yin thing I used the tither day? The plural of *yin* is *yin*.

Whar's yin things I used the tither day?

Interrogative Adjectives

Interrogative adjectives in English are 'what' and 'which'.

'What' is always pronounced *whit*.

'What time is it?' is expressed as:

Whit time is hid? Older people may be heard saying, *Whit o'clock is hid?*

Older people may also be heard using the forms *whitna*, *whitan* or *whitna fur a* for 'what'.

'What kind of thing is this that they are putting up at the end of the road?'

Whitna kinda thing is this thit thir pittan ap at the feet o the road?

'What man is that?'

Whitna fur a man is that? A reversed word order can also be heard:

Fur whitna man is that?

This is an appropriate place to point out that 'what' is used as an exclamation in English as in, 'What a lot you've got!' In Orkney dialect *whit* is used in a similar way. The above sentence would translate as, *Whit a lot yir gotten! Whitan* may also be used in this way but <u>not</u> *whitna. Whitan bonny flooers!*

Whitna and *whitan* are relics of obsolete English 'whatkin' = 'what kin' or 'what kindred'.

'Which' is used in the form *wheech* in Orkney dialect in this sense:
Wheech o this two bars o chocolate dae yi want?

The interrogative adjective *whit,* followed by *wan*, is much more commonly used:

Whit wan o this two bars* o chocolate dae yi want?

Adverbs

Verbs will be discussed in some detail presently. For the moment it is both convenient and logical to discuss adverbs. These tell us more about a verb. In the sentence, 'The man walked <u>quickly</u> across the road,' the adverb 'quickly' gives a more detailed description of his movement. By adding an 'ly' suffix many adjectives such as 'quick' can be changed into adverbs. In dialect the adjectival form of a word is frequently used instead of the adverb in which case:

'You would see him regularly in town' would take the form:
Yi wid see him in the toon reglar.
'I particularly like it.' is:
I like hid parteeclar.

Notice how these adjectives, when used as adverbs, prefer a position at the end of the sentence.

Here are other illustrations of the avoidance of adverbs. The English sentence, 'He carefully cut the wood in two,' might take the form:
He wir very carefil whin he cut the wid in two.
'She dances beautifully', might appear as:
She's a right bonny dancer.
'He foolishly took the money from the till', becomes:
He wir a right fool tae tak the money fae the till.

Adverbs of Place

Note the differences from Standard English:
For 'everywhere' use *everywey* or *everypiece.*

'He made friends everywhere he went':
He made freens everywey he gid*.
For 'nowhere' use *no wey* or *no piece*.
'The children had nowhere to play':
The bairns hid no piece tae play.
For 'somewhere' use *somewey* or *some piece*.
'I've seen that book lying somewhere'.
Ah'm seen that book lyan somewey.
'It will be lying somewhere.'
Hid'll be lyan some piece.
Note that *somewey* can also mean 'somehow'.
'He got out of it somehow or other':
He got oot o hid somewey ur ither.
For 'anywhere' use *anywey* or *any piece*.
'Have you seen my keys anywhere?'
Are yi seen me keys any piece?
Note that *anywey* can also mean 'anyway'!
'Anyway — he set off for town in the car . . . '
Anywey, he made fur the toon in the car . . .
A unique dialect adverb of place meaning 'near at hand' or 'nearby' is *aboot hands*.
A visitor to a house might enquire:
Is the man o the hoose aboot hands?
The Scots adverbs *ben* and *but* are still frequently used. *Ben* describes a movement towards the less frequently used rooms in a house. *But* is used for movement in the opposite direction. Note these examples:
(In the lounge) 'I think I must have left my glasses in the bedroom'.
I think I musta left me glesses ben.
(In the bedroom) 'I must remember to bring the hot water bottle through'.
I must mind on tae tak the hot watter bottle but.

* also '*geed*'

Adverbs of Time

'Now' is *noo* and Orcadians, unlike Scots, do not use the definite article in front of it. Scots may be heard to say 'the noo' or 'the now'. When an Orcadian loses his or her dialect this word, strangely enough, is one of the first to be modified and takes a form something akin to 'neow' in which the 'e' and 'o' are run together.

'Then' is pronounced *than* which means that, in certain circumstances, two consecutive 'than' forms can appear in a dialect sentence:

'Things were better then than they are now' will be spoken as:

Things wir better than than thir noo.

Afore and *ahint* are regularly used for 'before' and 'behind'.

'He had been home before'.

He wir been home afore.

'She was looking behind her the whole time'.

She wir lukkan ahint har the whole time.

English 'since' can be a Preposition, a Conjunction or an Adverb. In all instances Orkney dialect uses *fae* meaning 'from'. Here is an example of the adverbial use:

'He has never walked properly since he broke his ankle'.

He's niver waakèd right fae he broke his ankle.

Adverbs of Frequency

Affens is used for 'often'; it is in fact a contraction of English 'oftentimes'.

'Always' is pronounced *aalwis*.

Here are examples of usage:

Hid affens seems tae rain on a Thursday.

Yi'll aalwis see him at the Mart on a Monday.

Adverbs of Degree

Orcadians are very fond of adverbs of degree. Such adverbs modify adjectives or other adverbs. Dialect examples are *ferfil, aafil, terrible, horrible, horrid, dainty, gey, right, nearaboot, owerweel, rither, gret, kinda and kindaweys*. Here are some usages:

'He's done very well at university' translates as:

He's done ferfil weel at university.

'Very fine wedding, I'm told':

Aafil grand waddeen, thir tellan me.

'Terrible' and even 'horrible' can be used in the same way. An East Mainland mother spoke of a neighbour having a:

Horrible bonny bairn.

'This is really lovely cheese'.

This cheese is most horrid good.

'That's quite an acreage to plough'.

That's a dainty piece tae ploo.

'It's rather cold today'.

Hid's gey cowld the day.

'This jam is really good'.

This jam is right good.

Nearaboot is frequently used for 'nearly'.

I nearaboot gid heels ower head in the burn fur the stones wir ferfil slippy

An adverb unique to the dialect is *owerweel* which, when broken into its two elements, should mean 'very well'. In fact it means no more than 'well' or 'satisfactory'.

Hid's owerweel kent he's no tae be trusted. In this sentence *owerweel kent* means 'well known' but in a disparaging sense.

Ah'm no buyan a new coat, the owld wan'll deu owerweel. The verb *tae deu owerweel* means 'to be satisfactory.'

An amusing story is told about a dear Polish resident of Orkney who was well known throughout the county travelling around selling brushes and who picked up quite a bit of Orkney dialect. The pitfalls of learning a new language or dialect are shown by an exchange he had with one of his customers:

Customer: *Whit wey are thoo the day?*

Stanislaw: 'Very owerweel'.

Although dialect *owerweel* means merely 'well' it cannot be preceded by 'very'!

'Rather' is pronounced *rither*. It is frequently in use in sentences where Standard English speakers would use 'I prefer'. Here is an example:

'Do you prefer Australia?' *Na — I wad rither bide in Orkney.*

A nonsensical old Orkney riddle takes this form:

Whither wid yi rither or rither wid yi whither aet a stewed soo's snoot or a soo's snoot stewed? It means:

'Would you rather eat a stewed sow's snout or a sow's snout stewed?'!

Gret is frequently used to emphasise adjectives of 'size' or 'quality' as in:

He's biggan a gret big hoose, 'He's building a very large house'.

We saa him in his gret grand car yesterday, 'We saw him in his fine car yesterday'.

As in Scots, 'kind of' is pronounced *kinda* where it also means 'rather':

Hid's kinda cowld the day means 'It's rather cold today'.

Orkney dialect speakers also share with the Scots the word *kindaweys* which carries the same meaning:

'She's rather like her mother' may be expressed as:

She's kindaweys like her mither.

Interrogative Adverbs

In English these are 'how', 'where', 'when' and 'why'.

Dialect speakers use 'how' but pronounce it *hoo*.

'How much more land is that man going to buy?'

Hoo much more land is that man gan tae buy?

An interrogative adverbial phrase frequently used in Orkney dialect instead of *hoo* is *whit wey*.

'How do you do it?' can translate as:

Whit wey dae yi deu hid?

'How are you today?' can be expressed as:

Whit wey are thoo the day?

Whit like is a commonly used adverbial phrase, especially in the common greeting:

Whit like the day? meaning 'How are you today?' It is an abbreviated form of 'What do you feel like today?'

Returning to 'how', as can be seen, the pronunciation sounds exactly the same as the English pronunciation of 'who'. Fortunately in the dialect of Orkney the English relative pronoun and interrogative pronoun 'who' is not used (see under these separate sections).

'Where' is *whar*:

Whar are yi gan? is 'Where are you going?'

Whar is often followed by *piece* as in:

Whar piece are yi gan? That sentence also means merely, 'Where are you going?' In this instance 'piece' means 'place'.

Adults, before tickling a little child, say a teasing rhyme which begins:

> *Bore a holie, bore a holie,*
> *Whar piece, whar piece?*

See section under <u>Nouns</u> for more information on the use of 'piece' for 'place'.

A 'Who is Who?' book of Orkney celebrities should be entitled, *'Whar's Whar?'*! Notice that *whar* meaning 'where' is pronounced identically to *whar* meaning 'who':

Whar's gan whar? means 'Who's going where?'

An amusing local tale shows that even Orcadians can be confused with *whar* meaning 'where' and *whar* meaning 'who':

A rather simple minded Orkney man was walking home when he became enveloped in a dense sea-fog and totally lost his way. At last a house loomed in sight and not recognising it, he knocked on the door. When the *wife o the hoose* came to the door he asked, *'Whar am I?'* She looked at him and thinking he had lost his memory replied, *'Whar are thoo? Mercy–thoor Jock o the Quoys.'*

'When', as an interrogative adverb, is used exactly as in English and is pronounced in the same way. It is often followed by 'time'.

'When are you bringing in the cattle?'

When time are yi takkan the kye in?

Although 'when', as a question, meaning 'at what time?' is pronounced in the same way as in English, if it forms part of an adverbial clause, it is pronounced *whin*. This is a difficult distinction to grasp. Here is an illustration:

Speaker: *When are yi gan tae the toon?*

Listener: *Ah'm gan whin Ah'm ready.*

As can be seen from the illustration, *whin* is used when it means 'at a time when'.

Here is another illustration:

Whin I wir yir age I niver spok back tae a teacher.

'Why' is also used as in English. Older dialect speakers sometimes use *fur why*.

'He said he's leaving to go to Scotland/England tomorrow but he didn't tell me why'.

He said he's laevan fur sooth the morn bit he didna tell me fur why.

Sometimes the reversed form *why fur* can be heard, especially in response to a negative remark.

Speaker: 'I'm not going to my work tomorrow.'

Listener: 'Why not?'

These sentences might be expressed as:

Speaker: *Ah'm no gan tae me wark the morn.*

Listener: *Why fur no?*

Pronouns

A pronoun is used instead of a noun 1. to avoid repetition as for example in the English sentence 'When the dog was run over I immediately took <u>it</u> to the vet.' 2. where someone's name or the name of something is not known, 'Could <u>you</u> come this way please? 3. Where reference to a person or thing by the correct name would suggest inappropriate approval in the circumstances as in, 'Come out here <u>you</u>!' or 'Take <u>it</u> out of this room at once!' There is a considerable variety of pronouns:

<u>Subject Pronouns</u>

In English these are 'I', 'you' (singular), 'he', 'she', 'it', 'we', 'you' (plural') and 'they'.

Subject pronouns in Orkney dialect differ in several important ways. Orkney is one of the few parts of the English speaking world where the familiar form *thoo/thee* is still used:

'You know well enough the trouble that drink will cause.'

<u>*Thoo*</u> *kens weel enough the trouble thit drink'll caase.*

The pronoun 'he' was formerly used to describe the weather as in: *He's cowld the day*, a dialect rendering of 'It's cold today'.

'She' is often heard pronounced as *sheu* and is frequently used to describe inanimate things:

When fish weren't taking the bait, an old dialect nonsense utterance by fishermen was:

Sheu's nither a tistle ur a dochan i.e 'She is neither a thistle nor a dock'!

For third person singular 'it', Orcadians use *hid,* a form of Old English 'hit' which died out in England at the end of the 16th century!

'It's a really lovely day':
Hid's a right bonny day.
Where English uses the form, 'There's . . .' some Orcadians use the form *Hid's:*
'There's a little bit left in the bottom':
Hid's a gren left in the buddum.
'I' is pronounced as in English unless it is followed by 'am'. In such instances it is normally pronounced *ah* as in:
Ah'm thinkan aboot gittan a new television.
Where 'I' or 'am' are emphasised, 'I' is used as in English:
I am thinkan aboot gittan a new car.
'If you see any rats about the place let me know'.
If yi see any rats aboot the place lit me ken.
Where emphasis is required, 'you' is pronounced as in English:
Git oot o here — you!

Object Pronouns

In English these are 'me', 'you', him, 'her', 'it', 'us', 'you' (plural), 'them'.
In Orkney dialect such pronouns are *me, yi* (singular)*/thee, him/'im, har, hid/'id, iss, yi, them.*
Here are instances of usage:
'I saw you out at the clothes line the other day':
I saa thee oot at the claes line the tither day.
'I haven't seen him around for days':
Ah'm no seen 'im aboot hands fur days.
'I was told to bring her to the surgery immediately'.
I wis telt tae tak har tae the surgery right awey.
After a vowel, the initial *'hi'* of *hid* is lost unless emphasis is required:
Deu'd yirsel i.e. 'Do it yourself'.

'You have never seen us do that' becomes:

Yir niver seen <u>iss</u> deu that.

If emphasis is required *iss* takes the form *hiss*:

Yir niver seen <u>hiss</u> deu that.

For some strange reason *iss* can often be substituted for *me*. Orkney dialect speakers, in common with all English dialect speakers say *gimme* for 'give me' but *gaes,* a contracted form of *gae iss,* is also very commonly heard:

Gaes a gren more milk in me tea.

'If you're going to town will you take me with you?' may be expressed as:

If yir gan tae the toon will yi tak iss wi yi?

A most unusual use of the object pronouns *him* and *har* is found in Orkney dialect where they are combined as a noun in the form *him-har* and applied to any animal or person of indeterminate sex.

Possessive Pronouns

In English these are 'mine', 'yours (singular)', 'his', 'hers', 'its', 'ours', 'yours (plural)', 'theirs'.

In dialect they take the form:

Mine, yirs (singular)/*thine, his, hars, hids, wirs, yirs* (plural), *thirs.*

Since an 's' following an 'r' in dialect is pronounced 'sh', the pronouns above are sounded as 'harsh', 'wirsh', 'yirsh' and 'thirsh'.

'Are these glasses yours or mine?'
Is this glesses thine or mine?

Reflexive Pronouns

In English these are: 'myself', 'yourself', 'himself', 'herself', 'itself', 'ourselves', 'yourselves', 'themselves'.

In Orkney dialect the final 'f/ves' is lost and they take the form:
mesel, yirsel/theesel, himsel, harsel, hidsel, wirsels, yirsels, themsels/thirsels.

'You can do it yourself'.
Thoo can deu hid theesel.

Sometimes *me* can be heard substituted for *mesel*:

'I'll have to go and wash (myself) before I go out':
Ah'll hiv tae go and wash me afore I go oot.

'They have done it all themselves'.
Thir done hid aal thirsels: also Scots.

Demonstrative Pronouns

The demonstrative pronouns in English are 'this' and 'that' where they are associated with 'pointing out' an object. They are used in exactly the same way in Orkney dialect:
Luk at this!
I don't want that!

The plurals of 'this' and 'that' in English are 'these' and 'those'. These plurals are not used in Orkney dialect. Dialect speakers use instead the singular form:

'Whose trousers are these?' will be expressed as:
Whars breeks is this?

'What shoes are you going to have then?' 'I think I'll have these'. In such an instance Orkney dialect uses the singular form 'this' followed by *wans* in which case 'this' is used as a Demonstrative Adjective. Here is an example:

Whit shoes are yi gan tae hiv than? I think Ah'll hiv <u>this wans</u>.

Where English uses 'those' in this sense:

'Those who cannot pay now can bring the money tomorrow,' Orkney dialect substitutes the noun *fok* (i.e. 'folk'):

Fok thit canna pay noo can tak the money the morn.

'Them' may also be heard substituted for 'those' as shown in the old saying relating to the sanctity of the three small singing birds:

The laverock, the robin and the wren
<u>Them</u> thit kill that birds will never thrive again

Note that English 'these days' and 'those days' are expressed by *nooadays* and *thanadays*.

In the North Isles of Orkney the Demonstrative Pronoun *yin* is used for 'that'. Here is an example:

'Who is that walking down the road?'
Whar's yin waakan doon the road?

Relative Pronouns

In English the relative pronouns are 'that', 'who' and 'which'. It will be noticed that English uses 'that' not only as a demonstrative pronoun but also as a relative pronoun. In Orkney dialect the problem is simplified because whereas the demonstrative pronoun is pronounced 'that' as in English, the relative pronoun is always pronounced *thit*.

'That man that you see walking over there works on the pier with me':

<u>That</u> man <u>thit</u> yi see waakan ower there wirks on the pier wi me.

'Don't use the bucket that I keep for the ashes':

Don't use the bucket thit I keep fur the ashes.

In some instances the 'th' of *thit* is lost, in which case the first sentence above would read: *That man 'it yi see waakan ower there wirks on the pier wi me.*

The English relative pronouns 'who' and 'which' are not used in Orkney dialect; *thit* is used in every case.

<u>Interrogative Pronouns</u>

These pronouns usually appear at the beginning of a sentence in which a question is asked such as 'who,' 'which' and 'what'.

In the dialect of Orkney the interrogative pronoun 'who' is not used. The pronoun used to represent English 'who' is *whar*.

'Who is that standing over there?'

Whar's that stanan ower there?

Whars (notice different spelling) is used in place of 'whose'.

'Whose book is this lying on the floor?'

Whars book is this lyan on the floor?

Older people may be heard using the Scots form *wha* as in Scots 'Wha daur meddle wi me?' the usual translation of the Scots Latin motto 'Nemo me impune lacessit'.

'Which' is used in dialect as an interrogative pronoun and pronounced *wheech* but the Interrogative Adjective *whit,* followed by *wan*, is much more commonly used; see earlier under Interrogative Adjectives.

<u>The Pronoun 'one'</u>

The pronoun 'one', where the reference is to people, is not used in dialect. The English sentence, 'One needs to take care', would be transcribed as:

A buddy needs tae tak care.

'If one doesn't tell one the law, how is one supposed to know it?' becomes in Orkney dialect:

If a buddy disna tell a buddy the laa, hoo's a buddy supposed tae ken hid?

Notice that, in English, 'body' is used as a pronoun only when it has an adjective attached to it as in 'somebody', 'everybody', 'anybody' and 'nobody'. As can be seen, in Orkney dialect, it can be separated and used in the form *buddy*. In this sense it is the equivalent of English 'person':

Thir's an extra buddy fur tea the night.

Peggy can come in the car too — she's only a peedie buddy i.e a little person.

Dialect speakers do not use the pronouns 'someone', 'everyone', 'anyone' and 'no one', preferring the English alternatives 'somebody', 'everybody' 'anybody' and 'nobody'. The latter word can sometimes be heard in this form:

Thir's no a buddy aboot the hoose at aal meaning 'There's no one about the house at all'. Older people may be heard using the Scots form *aabody* for 'everyone'.

Notice that the plural of the pronoun *buddy* is *fok* = 'folk'.

The Pronouns 'little', 'much' and 'many'.

The English pronoun 'little' is generally not used in dialect. The English sentence:

'There was little to see' will be expressed as:

Thir wirna much tae see.

The English phrase 'little did he etc., know' however translates directly as *little did he ken.*

The pronoun 'a little' is invariably expressed as *a peedie gren.* Here is an exchange which shows the usage:

'How many sugars do you want?'

I jist tak a peedie gren.

Standard English uses 'much' as a pronoun as in 'We have much to do yet'.

Orkney dialect does not use 'much' positively in this sense. It would be expressed in dialect as:

We hiv a lot tae deu yit.

Oddly enough 'much' is used negatively as it is in English. Take this English example:

'There isn't much to do now' which takes a similar dialect form:

Thir's no much tae deu noo.

As in the case of 'much', 'many' is used negatively as an adjective:

Thir's no many tourists aboot noo.

Prepositions

The Scots prepositions *ahint, aside* and *atween* are used for 'behind', 'beside' and 'between'. The preposition *fornent*, an old Scots form of 'fore anent' and now rare in Scotland, is regularly used to mean 'in front of'. My neighbour asked me to 'tether the pony in front of the house the next day'. He said:

Fest the sholt the morn fornent the hoose.

Scots *abune*, above, used to be common in dialect but now may be heard spoken only by older people. It is found in the place-name *Abune the Hill* in Birsay. Other prepositions differ from standard English mainly in pronunciation. The table below shows the main differences:

English	Dialect
down	*doon*
for	*fur*
from	*fae*
into	*intae*
of	*o*
off	*off/aff*
onto	*ontae*
over	*ower*
to	*tae*
up	*up/ap*
with	*wi/wae*
without	*withoot*

Some illustrations of the use of dialect prepositions follow:

He's biggan a hoose <u>doon</u> the brae.

As can be seen from the table, 'for' is pronounced *fur*. Orkney parents had a number of sayings which they used when pestered by a questioning child. A common reply to *'Whit's that fur?'* was *'Cat's fur'*. Other common replies are much more rude!

Tak hid doon <u>fae</u> the shelf.

That bairn's <u>intae</u> everything.

Pit a gren <u>o</u> more milk in me tea, wid thoo.

Hid wir only whin the plane tuk <u>aff</u> thit I realised he wir tin the car keys wi him.

Ah'll git <u>ontae</u> the manager right awey.

He lives jist <u>ower</u> the brae.

<u>Up/ap</u> the hill I fand three teeo nests.

I saa har coman ap the street <u>wi</u> a great bag o messages.

I gid* tae the shop <u>withoot</u> money.

The preposition *tae* meaning 'to' can also be used in dialect with the meaning 'for':

Ah'll boil a egg <u>tae</u> yir tea.

He's wirkan <u>tae</u> the Orkney Builders noo.

Wid yi like me tae knit a jersey <u>tae</u> yi?

The preposition *tae,* when referring to time, means 'until':

Ah'll come the morn and Ah'll bide tae Tuesday.

Yir no gittan puddeen tae yi aet aal that maet.

Notheen more can go in the freezer tae I defrost hid.

Wantan is frequently used in dialect in the sense 'without'. It is the dialect Present Participle (see below) of English 'wanting' in the sense of 'lacking'. The sentence above could also be transcribed:

I gid tae the shop wantan money.

'Since' in English can be a Preposition, an Adverb or a Conjunction. In every case in dialect the word *fae* meaning 'from' is used. Here is an example of the use of *fae* as a preposition:

'I haven't seen him since the day I gave him a lift to town.'

Ah'm no seen him <u>fae</u> the day I gid him a lift tae the toon.

It should be noted that a characteristic of the dialect spoken

---

* also '*geed*'

by older people is the loss of the 'n' of the Preposition 'in' when that Preposition comes before the Definite Article 'the'. Here are some examples:

'Put it in the bag' becomes:

Pit hid i the poke.

'I saw you in town' will be expressed as:

I saa thee i the toon.

In all other instances the 'n' is retained. The loss of the 'n' before a Definite Article is also known in Scots.

Conjunctions

As the name suggests, conjunctions join two different ideas in a sentence. English 'also' is rarely used; *furbye* is usually substituted. Likewise, 'since', as a conjunction, is usually replaced by *fae*. Here are examples of dialect usage:

'He took the money out of the drawer and he also went away with my bank book'.

He tuk the money oot o the draaer and he gid awey wi me bank book furbye.

'I haven't seen him since he stole my money'.

Ah'm no seen him fae he stelt me money.

'Since' can also mean 'because' in English. When it means 'because' Orcadians frequently use the phrase *the wey* instead. 'He's probably got lost since he hasn't been here before' may be expressed as: *He's likely gotten lost the wey he's no been here afore.*

A few dialect conjunctions, like prepositions, differ mainly in pronunciation, the best examples being:

English	Dialect
but	*bit*
moreover	*furbye*
either	*ither*
however	*hooever/furtiver/furtiverweys*
or	*ur*
neither	*nither*
then	*than*

Here are examples of usage:

I used tae drive doon sooth bit nooadays I tak the plane.

He kam wi this grand praesent tae me and he hid wans tae the bairns furbye.

He didna come tae the waddeen — ither he wirna weel or we wir offended him.

He didna git intae the university he wanted; hooever he did git a place at Napier and he is right plaesed.

Furtiver is frequently used instead of *hooever. Furtiver* is a contraction of 'for whatever'. Unlike *hooever* which can be placed at the beginning or at the end of a sentence, *furtiver* is placed only at the end. Contrast:

Hooever he didna come or *He didna come hooever,* with:

He didna come furtiver.

Sometimes *furtiverweys* is substituted for *hooever.* It is a contraction of 'for whatever ways'. It can be used at the beginning or at the end of a sentence.

He said he wir gan tae come at seven. Furtiverweys he didna come.

Old people may be heard to say, *furtiverweys ur no* which carries the same meaning!

Here is an illustration from my own childhood. A visitor was describing some domestic situation where there had been some kind of problem. I cannot recall the details but he remarked, *Furtiverweys ur no me mither pat on the pot* which translates as, 'However my mother put the pot on (the fire)'.

Yi can waak intae the toon ur yi can tak the bike.

Hid's nither tae me or fae me. This old saying means, 'I don't mind either way'.

As in the case of 'then' used as an adverb of time, 'then' as a conjunction in Orkney dialect is pronounced *than.* In English it can be placed at the beginning or end of a question:

'What are you going to do then?' or 'Then — what are you going to do?' are both admissible.

In Orkney dialect 'than' as a conjunction always comes at the end of a sentence: *Whit are yi gan tae deu than?*

Verbs

Verbs are the building blocks of language. We cannot do very much without them. They describe actions or states in the present, in the past and in the future. What we have said on the subject of nouns is equally true of verbs in that some common English verbs are not used in Orkney dialect. English 'bring' in the sense, 'come with' for example is not used; the verb *tae tak* is substituted as in, *Tak the paeper ben whin yi come*. Strange to say the verb 'to bring up' in the sense of 'to rear' or 'to utter' is commonplace in all its tenses. *She browt up a big family.* The verb 'to become' likewise is not used; *tae git* i.e. 'to get' is substituted. 'He has become very conceited' would be expressed as *He's gotten ferfil bigsy*. English 'pick' is always used in preference to 'choose' which is rarely heard in dialect.

The verb 'to doubt' is used in interesting ways in Orkney dialect. In

I DOOT WIR IN FUR SOME
COORSE WATHER LASS

English 'to doubt' means 'to be undecided in opinion' but in Orkney dialect *tae doot* means 'to have an opinion about something negative':

'I think my car isn't going to pass its MOT' will be spoken as:
I doot me car's no gan tae pass hids MOT.

The verb *tae doot* is also used in reply to a negative idea where it carries the meaning 'I agree'.

A Standard English exchange between two speakers for example might take this form:

Speaker: It's going to rain.

Listener: I agree.

A similar exchange between two Orkney dialect speakers would take the form:

Speaker: *Hid's gan tae rain.*

Listener: *I doot hid.*

Compare remarks relating to the use of *widna* on p. 85.

Verbs can be 'regular', meaning that a great number of them follow the same rules of usage, or they can be 'irregular' in which case they follow no particular pattern. Let us begin with an example of a regular English verb which describes events at the present time. Such a verb is said to be in the Present Tense. We shall choose the verb 'to work'. When the verb appears in this form with a 'to' in front of it, it is said to be the Infinitive of the verb.

Present Tense

I work	we work
you (singular) work	you (plural) work
he works	they work
she works	
it works	

Notice that the verbal form changes only when 'he', 'she' or 'it' is used. In such cases an 's' is added to the verb. Now consider the same verb being used in Orkney dialect:

I wirk	*we wirk*
yi (singular) *wirk/thoo wirks*	*yi* (plural) *wirk*
he wirks	*they wirk*
she wirks	
hid wirks	

Notice that the form *thoo* surprisingly does not follow the form of *yi* but apparently follows the form of *he*, *she* and *hid*. This is a wrong assumption to make. *Thoo wirks* represents in fact obsolete English 'thou workst'.

Imperative of the Verb i.e. giving a Command

In English when we ask or order someone to do something for us we normally use the 'you' part of the verb without uttering 'you'. Here are examples:

'Take that from me'.

'Go now!'

'Think before you act!'

The verb 'to be' in Standard English is irregular. Although we say 'you are', we cannot say to a child 'Are good!', we have to say 'Be good!'

In the dialect of Orkney, commands are similar to those in Standard English but where the *thoo* form is used there is a very distinct difference. To lift a long heavy batten a workman asked me to take one end and he would take the other. He spoke in dialect:

Thee tak the wan end and Ah'll tak the tither.

He may also have said:

Tak thee the wan end and Ah'll tak the tither.

Notice that *thoo* is not used as expected but *thee* and the form of the verb is also different. *Thee* is normally heard only as an object pronoun (see below) but in commands, for some unexplained reason, it is also used as a subject pronoun:

Here are some other examples:
Go thee there and watch.
Wait thee here a meenitie.
Git thee oot o here at wance!

Readers familiar with Orkney dialect may form the impression that there is another form of command using the *thoo* form when they hear such phrases as:
Luks thoo!

This is apparently an instruction 'to look'. This phrase really means 'Are you looking?' and is a contraction of obsolete English 'Lookest thou?'

Later, reference will be made to the use of *Sistoo!* in former times. It was also used to mean *Look!* but it is really a contracted form of obsolete English 'Seest thou?', i.e. 'Do you see?'

The negative form of the <u>Present Tense</u> in English normally requires the introduction of the verb 'to do':

I don't work	we don't work
you (singular) don't work	you (plural) don't work
he doesn't work	they don't work
she doesn't work	
it doesn't work	

The negative form of the <u>Present Tense</u> in Orkney dialect is:

I don't wirk	*we don't wirk*
yi (singular) don't wirk/thoo disna wirk	*yi (plural) don't wirk*
he disna wirk	*they don't wirk*
she disna wirk	
hid disna wirk	

The *na* suffix of the verb becomes 'not' if emphasis is required.

The verb 'to do' is also used in the construction of questions in Standard English:

do I work?   do we work?
do you (singular) work?   do you (plural) work?
does he/she work?   do they work?
does it work?

In dialect, questions normally take this form:

dae I wirk?   *dae we wirk?*
dae yi (singular)/*dis thoo wirk?* *dae yi* (plural) *wirk?*
dis he/she wirk?   *dae they wirk?*
dis hid wirk?

This is an appropriate place to point out that the rarer form of question in which the pronoun *thoo* and the verb are reversed, can also be heard with several of the more common verbs:
'Do you know the man who lives in the house at the shore?'
Kens thoo the man thit lives in the hoose at the shore?
'What do you think?'
Whit thinks thoo?
'Do you see that house on the hilltop?'
Sees thoo the hoose on the tap o the brae?
As we have shown earlier, *Sees thoo* can be found abbreviated to *sistoo* in old dialect writing where it meant *Look!*

In Orkney dialect 'to do' is pronounced in three ways according to the situation. These are *deu*, *dae* and, as in English, 'do'. In dialect questions *dae* is always used, never *deu* or 'do'.
Notice this example:
Whit kinda wark <u>dae</u> yi <u>deu/do</u>?
<u>Dae</u> yi think I could <u>deu/do</u> hid?

Unusual variants of the negative in dialect are associated with the verb *tae ken*. Instead of saying *I don't ken* meaning 'I don't know', a dialect speaker can be heard saying *I ken no*, a sentence which is often run together as *I kinno*. Where elderly dialect speakers pronounce the initial 'k' as 'ty' this will be sounded as *I tyinno*. The English sentence 'Goodness knows for I don't know (the answer)' is expressed succinctly in dialect as *Bes tyens fur I tyinno*. Another variant of the negative of the verb *tae ken* may be heard in the peculiar idiom *Niver a ken I* meaning 'I don't know'. The function of the 'a' here is not understood; it must have some function since it is impossible to use this phrase without it. There is another reversal of the verb and the pronoun in the phrase *Ken I no!* with emphasis on the '*no*' which does not mean 'I do not know', as might be expected. In fact it means the very opposite. It means 'I most certainly know'!

The most commonly used verbs in English are irregular. Take the verb 'to be' in the <u>Present Tense</u> as an example:

I am (I'm) we are (we're)
you (singular) are (you're) you (plural) are (you're)
he is (he's) they are (they're)
she is (she's)
it is (it's)

This verb is so irregular that the word 'be' does not appear in any part of it although it can be heard in English dialects as for example, 'Oi be the fourth generation in this farm.'

Notice that this verb is severely contracted in English usage as the forms in brackets show. The verb *tae be* becomes even more contracted in the dialect of Orkney:

Ah'm *wir*
yir (singular)/*thoor** *yir* (plural)
he's *thir*
she's
hid's

* *although yir* is a contraction of 'you are', *thoor* is a contraction of obsolete English 'thou art'

If a plural noun is used instead of the plural pronoun 'they', the singular form of the verb 'to be' is often heard as in this imaginary exchange:

'Thir on the table'.
'Whit's on the table?'
'The books is on the table'.

Here are more examples:

Hurry up — the men's here already.
Things is made* far too complicated the day.

Standard English 'there are' does not take the plural form in Orkney dialect:

Thir's weeman stanan ootside the door here waitan.
Thir's times when I wish I niver mov'd tae the toon.

The use of the singular part of the verb with a plural noun is very common in English dialects. Such usage is considered extremely bad (Standard) English!

Where the pronoun or the verb is emphasised, the normal English pattern is followed in Orkney dialect e.g.

'I am sick of hearing you moaning' is:

I am seek o hearan yi moanan.

In the negative form of the verb *tae be*, all 'nots' become 'no', as in *Ah'm no, yir no* etc., but again, where emphasis is required, the normal English pattern is followed:

'I am not letting you out in this wet (weather)' is:

I am not littan yi oot in this weet.

Another commonly used irregular verb in English is the verb 'to have':

I have	we have
you (singular) have	you (plural) have
he has	they have
she has	
it has	

* also *'meed'*

The Orkney dialect version is also irregular:

I hiv/hae	*we hiv/hae*
yi (singular) *hiv/hae:thoo his/haes*	*yi* (plural) *hiv/hae*
he his/haes	*they hiv/hae*
she his/haes	
hid his/haes	

The *hae* forms are used only by older people.

The negative forms are:
I hivna etc/I hinna etc. or *I don't hiv/I don't hae* etc.
In English there are two forms of the Present Tense, the Simple Present as above and the Continuous Present which describes an ongoing action. Let us take the verb 'to fish' to show the differences between the two tenses in English usage:

Simple Present

'I fish in the loch on Saturdays'.

Continuous Present

'I'm fishing in the loch now'.

As can be seen the Continuous Present is made up of the Present Tense of the verb 'to be' and what is called the Present Participle of the verb 'to fish' which is formed by adding 'ing' to it. Other examples are 'wishing', 'doing', 'walking' etc. Sometimes the verb ending has to be modified; the final 'e' for example is usually dropped. 'Hope' becomes 'hoping'. Sometimes the final consonant has to be doubled as in the case of 'hop' which becomes 'hopping'.
The Simple Present takes this form in Orkney dialect:

I fish in the loch on Setterdays and the negative form is:
I don't fish in the loch on Setterdays.

The <u>Continuous Present</u> takes this form:

Ah'm fishan in the loch noo and the negative is:
Ah'm no fishan in the loch noo.

The Present Participle

Fishan is the Present Participle of the verb 'tae fish' in Orkney dialect. All Present Participles in Orkney dialect are formed by adding *an* and not 'ing' to the infinitive. This creates a problem in the written form of Orkney dialect where some infinitives end in 'e', the best example being the verb *tae be*. In theory the Present Participle should be *bean* but since this forms another English word the result could be confusing. The Present Participle of the verb *tae be* has to be hyphenated and take the form *be-an*. Standard English is faced with similar problems. Normally the final 'e' of an infinitive is dropped to form the Present Participle as in the case of 'hope' above. In the case of the English verb 'to singe', dropping the final 'e' would give the Present Participle 'singing' but to avoid confusion with the verb 'to sing', the 'e' is retained in 'singeing'. English also retains the final 'e' of 'to be' in the Present Participle otherwise 'being' would be written 'bing'. There is a tendency in Orkney dialect to drop a final 'd' if it follows an 'n'. As an example, 'and' is frequently pronounced *an*. 'Stand' is pronounced *stan* and the Present Participle is *stanan* or *stannan*. An old house in Flotta was called *Stannanstone*, i.e. 'standing stone'.

Since dialect Present Participles are formed from the infinitive of the dialect verb, many dialect Present Participles look different from their English equivalents. Below are some of the more irregular Present Participles:

English Present Participle	Orkney Dialect Present Participle
falling	*faan*
giving	*gae-an*
going	*gan*
holding	*haddan*
knowing	*kennan*

An interesting dialect Present Participle is *gittan* i.e. 'getting' used in the sense of 'becoming'. This participle, unlike other Present Participles can be placed at the end of a sentence. Notice the difference between Standard English and Orkney dialect in this example in which a dialect speaker is talking about her cat:

'It never hunts; I think I'm giving it too much food; it's becoming a big, fat cat'.

Hid niver fends; I think Ah'm gae-an hid too much maet; hid's a big, fat cat noo gittan.

In Orkney dialect as in English, the Present Participle is used in the Continuous Present but notice the difference:

'I am sitting here wishing that you were with me' becomes:

Ah'm sittan here wishan thit yi wir wi me.

Here are other examples:

'He's saying that he's only drinking water tonight'.

He's sayan thit he's only drinkan watter the night.

'One can watch television and be knitting at the same time'.

A buddy can watch television and be knittan at the sam time.

An interesting aspect of the dialect of Orkney is the frequent use of two Present Participles in a sentence, both conveying the same idea, with one immediately following the other! Here are examples of this usage:

Standard English, 'It's pouring with rain' is expressed in dialect as:

Hid's pooran and rainan.

'That kettle on the Aga is boiling furiously' is:

That kettle on the Aga is rampan and boilan.

BOGLAN AND GREETAN

'The child was crying his eyes out', will be expressed as:

The bairn wir boglan and greetan.

'I saw him smirking behind my back' could take the form:

I saa him cheeteran and laughan ahint me back.

Future Tense

The Future Tense differs very little from English and needs only one example:

Ah'll fish   *we'll fish*
yi'll fish/thoo'll fish   *yi'll fish*
he'll fish   *they'll fish*
she'll fish
hid'll fish

Notice that, as in the case of the verb *tae be*, the pronoun 'I' takes the form *Ah*.

The negative form of such verbs is *Ah'll no fish, yi'll no fish* etc. The English forms 'won't' and 'shan't' are not used in dialect.

English has another type of <u>Future Tense</u> in which the verb 'to go' is used in the <u>Present Continuous Tense</u> followed by the active verb in the <u>Infinitive</u>. Here is an example:

'I am going to fish tomorrow'. In Orkney dialect this sentence is expressed in the form:

Ah'm gan* tae fish the morn. The negative form is:
Ah'm no gan tae fish the morn.

It is useful to introduce this form of the <u>Future Tense</u> here because it also helps to show that *gan,* the <u>Present Participle</u> of the verb *tae go* in dialect, looks very irregular. It is in fact a contracted form of *go-an*, i.e. 'going'. Notice the Orkney idiom *Had gan!* which translates as 'Off you go!' (but it isn't with my blessing).

<u>Conditional Tense</u>

The Conditional Tense in English is used where someone may do something <u>if</u> some other condition is satisfied and nearly always includes the word 'would' as in *I would fish, he would fish* etc.

In dialect, 'would' is pronounced *wid* or, by older people *wad*:

* also '*gaan*'

*He wid fish if he hid a rod** and the negative is *He widna fish*
. . . but notice how the word order changes when this takes the
form of a question:

'Wouldn't he fish if he had a rod?' would be expressed in
dialect as *Wid he no fish if he hid a rod?*

A popular phrase in dialect to express certainty is *Wad*
I/thoo/he etc no!

Wad thoo stop wirkan if thoo kam intae money? Wad I no!

Past Tense

The Past Tense in English, like the Present Tense takes
several different forms:

1. Simple Past

In the Simple Past the verb describes an action or experience
in the past as in:

'I took my tablets this morning' or 'I felt quite sick when I
saw the state of the house'.

In the case of regular verbs the simple past is formed by
adding 'ed' to the infinitive. The simple past of 'to fish' for
example is 'fished' as in 'Yesterday I fished in the loch'.

The final 'ed' of the Simple Past is sounded in English after
the consonants 'd' and 't' as in 'loadèd' and 'twistèd'. In Orkney
dialect the 'ed' of the Simple Past is often sounded too after 'b',
'g', 'k' and 'p' as in *robbèd, waggèd, likèd* and *jumpèd.*

Many English verbs have irregular simple past forms. Look
at the above sentences 'I took my tablets this morning' and 'I felt
quite sick when I saw the state of the house'. 'Took' is the simple
past form of 'take' and 'felt' is the simple past form of 'feel'.
Orkney dialect follows many of the irregular forms of English
Simple Past but it also has developed some irregular forms. Here
is a table which shows the main differences:

* pronounced '*rode*' in dialect

Infinitive of Verb	English Simple Past	Orkney Dialect Simple Past
catch	caught	*catched*
chase (Ork. *chaest*)	chased	*chaested*
come	came	*kam*
creep	crept	*creepèd*
draw (Ork. *draa*)	drew	*draa'd*
drive	drove	*drave*
droond (Eng. 'drown')	drowned	*droonded*
find=	found	*fand/fund*
freeze	froze	*freezed*
flee (Eng. 'fly')	flew	*fled/fleed*
give (Ork. *gae*)	gave	*gid/geed*
go	went	*gid*
greet (Eng. 'weep')	——	*gret*
have (Ork. *hiv*)	had	*hid*
hear	heard	*hard*
hold (Ork *had/howld*)	held	*hadded/held*
hit	hit	*hat*
keep	kept	*keepèd*
know (Ork. *ken*)	knew	*kent*
let (Ork. *lit*)	let	*lit*
put (Ork. *pit*)	put	*pat/pot*
rive (Eng. 'tear')	——	*rave*
sell	sold	*selt*
shit (Ork. *shite+*)	shit	*shat/shet*
steal (Ork. *stael*)	stole	*stelt/staeled*
start (Ork. *stert*)	started	*stert**
strike (Ork. *strick*)	struck	*strack*
swell (Ork. *swaal*)	swelled	*swaaled*
take (Ork. *tak*)	took	*tuk*
teach	taught	*teached*
tell	told	*telt*
wash	washed	*wush*
wet (Ork. *weet*)	wet	*weetèd*
wind=	wound	*wund*
work (Ork. *wirk*)	worked	*wirked/wrowt*

= rhyme with 'wind(ow)'.   + vulgar

* This is a most interesting verb since the Present Tense, the Simple Past and the Perfect Tense are all the same e.g. I stert next Monday; I stert last Friday; Ah'm stert already. There are a few such verbs in English e.g. 'cut' and 'set'.

HE'S FERFIL FUR CHAESTAN CATS

Notice that, although the <u>verb</u> 'work' is pronounced *wirk** in dialect; the <u>noun</u> 'work' is always pronounced *wark*. The Orkney dialect phrase *tae wirk a wark* means to 1. play tricks, as at Hallowe'en 2. to behave in an odd way e.g. of an engine 3. to be extremely busy, usually in the making of something.

The verb *tae bide* meaning 'to stay' is common in Orkney dialect. It is found in Scots too but not in Standard English. It has the irregular past tense *bade*:

He bade in Orphir a whilie wi his mither.

The <u>Simple Past</u> of the verb 'to be' in English is quite irregular:

I was	we were
you (singular) were	you (plural) were
he was	they were
she was	
it was	

Notice the difference in the <u>Simple Past</u> of the Orkney verb *tae be*:

I wir/wis	*we wir*
you (singular) wir/thoo wir	*you (plural) wir*
he wir/wis	*they wir*
she wir/wis	
he wir/wis	
hid wir/wis	

* also '*wurk*'

The English sentence 'I was going to go but I fell ill' translates into Orkney dialect as:

I wir gan tae go bit I tuk no weel.

'It was a lovely day when we left to go to cut peat ' reads as:

Hid wir a bonny day whin we left fur the paet hill.

The '*I wir*', '*he/she/hid wir*' forms which are also found in English dialects are in a stage of transition today. For the sake of consistency all the examples in the book use the '*wir*' form.

Past Continuous

This verbal form relates to a 'snapshot' of an ongoing action in the past and in Standard English uses the verb 'to be' in the Past Tense with the <u>Present Participle</u>. It is really odd that the <u>Present Participle</u> is used to describe an action in the past! It is for this reason that some authorities do not use the term <u>Present Participle</u> but use instead the term <u>Active Participle</u>. The approach used in this book is to adopt the term Present Participle rather than Active Participle since this is the term favoured by most authorities. Here are examples of the use of the <u>Present Participle</u> in the <u>Past Continuous</u>:

'He was fishing when I saw him last' and the negative form is:

'He wasn't fishing when I saw him last'.

Orkney dialect uses a similar form:

He wir fishan whin I saa him last and the negative form is:

He wirna fishan whin I saa him last.

Narrative Past Tense

In Standard English the Simple Present Tense is often used to describe events in the past in which the speaker has been involved or has witnessed and is frequently used by writers. Here is an example from Standard English in which there is someone listening intently to what happened when her friend, on holiday, had a puncture on the motorway:

Listener: 'Goodness, what did you do?'

Speaker: 'I get the car on to the hard shoulder, I open the boot, take all the luggage out, get out the spare wheel and just at that moment a police car pulls up behind me . . . '

As the reader can see the speaker uses the Present Tense to describe an event that has happened in the past. There is no special name for this tense in English since it is exactly the same as the Simple Present Tense.

In Orkney dialect, when a speaker relates such an incident he uses a completely original tense which I shall call the Narrative Past Tense. It also exists in Scots and English dialect:

Here is the Narrative Past tense of the verb *tae go*:

I goes	*we goes*
you (singular) *goes/thoo goes*	*you* (plural) *goes*
he goes	*they goes*
she goes	
hid goes	

Notice that the Third Person Singular of the Present Tense is used for all of the Narrative Past Tense. The forms *you/thoo goes* would be used only extremely rarely in an instance where both the speaker and the listener had been involved in an event which the speaker was recalling.

Here are examples of dialect usage:

'Weel hid wir like this: the man said I hid tae wait so <u>*I sits*</u> *doon . . . '.*

'He telt me he couldna help iss so <u>*we goes*</u> *oot . . . '.*

Reversal of normal word order is frequently associated with this tense:

'*He comes oot o this car haddan sometheen and <u>thinks I</u> tae mesel, is hid a gun?'*

<u>*Says I*</u> *tae him, 'Yi'll no be takkan the bairns wi yi?'*

Not all verbs in Orkney dialect use the Narrative Past Tense; exceptions are for example the verbs *tae be, tae hiv* and *tae ken* which use the Present Tense.

Perfect Tense

This tense describes what you have done, what you have felt or what has happened. Such tenses use the verb 'to have' along with a <u>Past Participle</u> of the verb which is normally formed by adding 'ed' to the infinitive or simply 'd' if the verb ends in 'e'. The <u>Perfect Tense</u> of the verb 'to fish' is 'fished':

'I have fished.' and the Perfect Tense of 'hope' is: 'I have hoped'.

Unfortunately English has many irregular Past Participles and Orkney dialect also has irregular forms:

Infinitive of Verb	English Past Participle	Orkney Dialect Past Participle
bide (Eng. 'stay')	———	*bidden*
catch	caught	*catched*
come	come	*comed*
draa (Eng. 'draw')	drawn	*draa'd*
drink	drunk	*drukken*
droond (Eng. 'drown')	drowned	*droonded*
fa (Eng. 'fall')	fallen	*faan*
find*	found	*fund*
flee (Eng. 'fly')	flown	*fleed*
get (Ork. *git*)	got	*gotten*
give (Ork. *gae*)	given	*gin/geen/gaen*
go	gone	*gin*
have (Ork. *hiv/hae*)	had	*hin*
hear	heard	*hard*
hit	hit	*hitten*

* rhyme with 'wind(ow)'

Infinitive of Verb	English Past Participle	Orkney Dialect Past Participle
knit	knit	*knitten*
know (Ork. *ken*)	known	*kent*
let (Ork. *lit*)	let	*litten*
meet	met	*mitten*
put (Ork. *pit*)	put	*pitten*
sell	sold	*selt*
shit+ (Ork. *shite*)	shit	*shitten*
sit	sat	*sitten*
steal (Ork. *stael*)	stolen	*stelt*
start (Ork. '*stert*')	started	*stert*
strike (Ork. *strick*)	struck	*stricken*
teach	taught	*teached*
take (Ork. *tak*)	taken	*tin/teen*
tell	told	*telt*
wind*	wound	*wund*

        * rhyme with 'wind(ow)'
        + vulgar

Notice the tendency to use the old suffix 'en' in the Past Participle. American English continues to use 'gotten'. Orkney shares with Scots the Past Participle 'pitten'. A pupil who was asked by a teacher to comment on an error in the work of another child is alleged to have said, *He's gin and pitten 'pitten' whar he shoulda pitten 'put'.*

The Past Participle of the verbs *tae go* and *tae gae* are the same in dialect.

English 'I have gone and given him it' translates into dialect as:

    Ah'm gin* and gin+ him hid.

In the use of the Perfect Tense, Orkney and Shetland dialect differ completely from Standard English. In fact it is one of the

* also '*geen*'
+ also '*gaen*'

most fundamental differences. Where English uses the verb 'to have' along with the Past Participle to express the Perfect Tense, Orkney and Shetland dialect use the verb *tae be*.

English, 'I have seen her,' takes this form in Orkney dialect:
Ah'm seen har.
Here are some other dialect examples:
Ah'm been there afore. (I have been . . .)
Thoor tin some ferfil bonny photos. (You (singular) have taken . . .)
Thir affens helpèd iss oot in bad wather. (They have often . . .)
Wir telt yi aal wi hiv tae tell. (We have told . . .)
Ah'm hin me breakfast. (I have had . . .)
Negative forms are:
Ah'm no seen har.
Ah'm no been . . .

With some verbs in the spoken dialect there can be confusion over whether something is happening in the present or has happened in the past. This happens only when the Present Participle of the verb and the Past Participle sound similar. Consider this English sentence:
'I have knitted a pair of socks today'. In dialect this reads:
Ah'm knitten a pair o socks the day. Contrast this with:
Ah'm knittan a pair o socks the day.
The former means, 'I have knitted . . . and the latter means 'I am knitting . . . !
This only happens where some Past Participles end in *en*. Here is another example:
Contrast:
Ah'm litten the cat oot with:
Ah'm littan the cat oot.
The former states that the cat 'has been let out' and the latter that the cat 'is being let out'!

The Past Participle and Present Participle of *tae faa*, to fall, are the same:

Hid's faan doon can mean 'It's falling down' or 'It has fallen down'! Perhaps the reader can see the humour in this dialect conversation:

Child: Mither–the picture's faan doon aff the waal!

Mother: Weel–catch hid than!

Future Perfect Tense

This tense is used when there is an expectation that something has happened e.g. a guest says to a visitor, 'You'll have seen the trees which I planted?' It may also be used when there is an expectation that something will happen, 'When you see the trees I planted, by then you'll have seen all the changes.' In Orkney dialect 'have' is omitted in the Future Perfect in which case the guest would say, *Yi'll seen the trees I planted?* or *Whin yi see the trees I planted, bi than yi'll seen aal the changes.* Since, as already pointed out, 'shan't' and 'won't' are not used in Orkney dialect, the negative forms are quite different from Standard English. 'You won't have seen the trees I planted,' becomes, *Yi'll no seen the trees I planted.*

Conditional Perfect Tense

This requires the use of the so-called Auxiliary Verbs such as 'should', 'would', and 'could'. A special section is devoted to these later. Auxiliary Verbs are used in English along with the Perfect Tense to express some condition other than what occurred in the past. Such usage is called the Conditional Perfect. Here are some examples:

'He could have been swept out to sea'.

'He should have been there'.

'He would have stayed at home if . . .'

Although Orkney dialect uses the verb *tae be* and not the verb *tae hiv* in the Perfect Tense, in the Conditional Perfect *tae hiv* is used but not the form *hiv* as might have been expected. The simple word '*a*' is used and is attached to the auxiliary word! The sentences above translate into Orkney dialect as:

He coulda been swept oot tae sea.
He shoulda been there.
He wida/wada bidden home if . . .

Similar forms are found in other English dialects.

In Orkney dialect *wida/wada* is often used without the final '*a*' as in:

He wid/wad bidden home . . .

Here are other examples:

She wid/wad hitten him if he hin said anither wird.
He wid/wad died if they hinna fund him.

An interesting thing happens in the negative forms of *coulda, shoulda* and *wida*. The reader will remember that the negative forms of *could, should* and *wid* are *couldna, shouldna* and *widna* and therefore in the sentence *He coulda been swept oot tae sea* we would expect the negative form to be:

He couldna a been swept oot tae sea with the 'a' representing *hiv* immediately following the 'a' of *couldna*. In practice the first 'a' wipes out the second and the negative form is therefore:

He couldna been swept oot tae sea which means, 'He could not have been swept out to sea.'

The other examples are:

He shouldna been there.
He widna bidden home (even) if . . .

See also a reference to the Conditional Tense in Pluperfect Tense below.

PLOO PERFECT?

<u>Pluperfect Tense</u>

This tense tells you what happened in the past before something else happened. Such tenses can be recognised in English by the word 'had' in them and often have the words 'before' or 'after' in them:

'After <u>he had finished</u> he went out.'

Notice that Pluperfect Tense is expressed by the Past Tense of the verb 'to have' and the Past Participle. Here is another example:

<u>She had waited</u> for an hour before he turned up.

In Orkney dialect the Pluperfect Tense like the Perfect Tense is expressed, not by the Past Tense of the verb 'to have' and the Past Participle but by the Past Tense of the verb *tae be* and the Past Participle.

'He had gone out of the shop before me . . .' takes the form:

He wir gin oot o the shop afore me . . .

'They had had many people staying' translates as:

They wir hin a lot o fok bidan.

The negative forms are:

He wirna gin . . . which means, 'He had not gone . . .'

They wirna hin . . . meaning, 'They had not had . . .'

As in the case of the Simple Past Tense, the Pluperfect Tense is in a stage of transition too and the forms *I'd been, he'd been* etc., are frequently heard in dialect today.

Notice the strange thing which happens however when the word 'if' is introduced in these sentences:

If he hin gin oot o the shop afore me . . .

If they hin hin a lot o fok bidan . . .

In these instances the verb *tae hiv* is used instead of the verb *tae be!* The reason for the change is that the word 'if' introduces a condition in which case the sentence requires the use of a Conditional Tense.

Here is another example; firstly the English sentence:

'If I had known you were coming, I would have met you; now the dialect translation:

If I hin kent yi wir coman I wad mitten yi.

Perfect Continuous Tense and Pluperfect Continuous Tense

In English these take the forms:

'I have been fishing all day' and 'I had been fishing all day . . .'.

In Orkney dialect these follow rules which have already been explained and appear in these forms:

Ah'm been fishan aal day.

The negative form is:

Ah'm no been fishan . . .

I wir been fishan aal day whin aal o a sudden . . .

The negative form is:

I wirna been fishan . . .

The Gerund

Apart from the striking difference between Orkney dialect and Standard English in the formation of the Perfect and Pluperfect Tenses, Orkney dialect has another unique characteristic. Let us return to the English Present Participle and take as an example 'fishing' as in:

'He's fishing'.

It was noted that this took the form:

He's fishan in dialect.

Although the form 'fishing' is not used in this sense, 'fishing' is used in dialect in another sense. Take the English sentence:

'I like fishing'.

The Orkney dialect version is:

I like fisheen.

This is because in this instance 'fishing' is really a noun made from the verb. This special noun is called a <u>Gerund</u>. Generally in Orkney dialect the final 'ing' is almost always pronounced 'een'. This produces some interesting differences between the dialect of Orkney and Standard English:

'I go fishing because I like fishing' becomes in dialect:

I go fishan becaes I like fisheen.

'He's been farming in Aberdeenshire for years and I'm told his son is going to take up farming now' will be expressed in this way:

He's been ferman in Aberdeenshire fur 'ears and thir sayan his son is gan tae tak up fermeen noo.

'We are taking a lot of money in; when we have finished I'll count the takings' reads as:

Wir takkan a lot o money in; whin wir feeneeshed Ah'll coont the takkeens.

'What a job we had parking the car for there was just no parking to be had.'

Whit a job we hid parkan the car fur thir wir jist no parkeen tae be hin.

'We have been waiting for hours; I don't like all this waiting' is expressed as:

Wir been waitan fur 'oors; I don't like aal this waiteen.

'I saw you making a bride's cog; there's a lot of work in the making of it' reads:

I saa yi makkan a bride's cog; thir's a lot o wark in the makkeen o hid.

FETH HID IS A GOOD COG

Dialect Gerund

The use of the Gerund in Orkney dialect is one of the most difficult aspects to grasp correctly. In Standard English it is used in many instances. Its uses in Orkney dialect are quite specific:

1. It is used where it acts as a noun describing an activity or instruction with or without the definite article or indefinite article in front of it:

Thir's a <u>meeteen</u> in the school the night.

The <u>painteen</u> o the windows is no feeneeshed yit.

Dae yi ever go tae the <u>danceen</u>?
That bairns'll no tak a <u>telleen</u> (they won't behave)
Thir's a <u>warneen</u> aboot bad weather.
2. It is used where it acts as a noun relating to an activity
which one could see on a sign
Thir seems tae be wirkeen gan on at the quarry the day.
(DANGER: QUARRY WORKING)
Thir's sweemeen in the pool every efternoon fur owld fok.
(SWIMMING TODAY)
He wir knockèd doon on the crosseen. (PLEASE USE
ZEBRA CROSSING)
She's hopan tae mak a career in acteen. (ACTING
COURSES AVAILABLE)
3. It is used as an adjective <u>in compound nouns</u> such as:
plumbeen wark, diveen board, fisheen boat, walkeen stick,
skippeen rope, steereen wheel, runneen track—where they mean
'in connection with' plumbing, diving, walking, running etc.
'Man-eating shark' in English is ambiguous when spoken.
One can see a man-eating shark off the coast of Australia or a
man eating shark in a restaurant today. There is no such
ambiguity in the dialect of Orkney. An Orcadian would see a
man-eateen shark off the Australian coast indeed but in the
restaurant he would see a *man eatan* shark!
4. Where a noun describes a specific object such as a
'painting', a 'dwelling', a 'building' etc., then the gerund is used.
A good rule of thumb is that if the gerund can be made plural,
then it is used in dialect.
Hid wir winderfil min tae see the wirkeens o the computer-
controlled milkeen machine.
5. A gerund is never used in front of a preposition in dialect.
Ah'm no very keen on cyclan.
I canna go a bike withoot faan aff.
Yi should aalwis hiv a shooer efter sweeman.

Ah'm lukkan forward tae meetan him. Contrast that with
Ah'm lukkan forward tae wir meeteen.

6. A gerund is not used if it immediately follows a verb:

Me faither loved wirkan in the paet hill.

He suggested gan tae the toon.

I didna mind helpan the man.

A caveat has to be added to this study of the Gerund in
Orkney dialect. The people on the islands of Burray and South
Ronaldsay do not make the distinction between the Present
Participle and the Gerund. Whereas Orcadians generally would
say, *Ah'm been fishan fur I like fisheen,* a native of these islands
would say, *Ah'm been fishan fur I like fishan.* The native Gerund
in which 'ing' forms are used do not apply in these islands.

This is an appropriate point to discuss the pronunciation of all
words in dialect which end in 'ing' but are not formed from
verbs. Generally they are pronounced in the same way as the
Gerund but there are several inconsistencies. Although 'thing'
and 'everything' are pronounced as in English, 'something' is
pronounced *sometheen* and 'nothing' is pronounced *notheen.*
There are several dialect adverbs of motion ending in 'lings'
which follow the above pronunciation such as *backleens* 'going
backwards', *halfleens* 'half way', *twartleens* 'across' and
erseleens, 'moving backside first'.

Auxiliary Verbs

There are several verbs in English called Auxiliary Verbs. These odd verbs which have no infinitive forms can only be used to 'help' other verbs. Those we are concerned with here are 'should/would', 'may/might', 'can' and 'could'. 'May' is not used as a verb in Orkney dialect, only the derived word 'maybe' which takes the form *mibbe* in dialect. It is frequently used in a sentence where Standard English would use 'may' or 'might'.

'I may go tomorrow' translates best as:

Ah'll mibbe go the morn the negative form of which is:

Ah'll mibbe no go the morn.

'Might' can also be used as in:

We might tak the kye in on Monday but the preferred negative form would be;

We'll mibbe no tak the kye in on Monday.

In dialect 'can' is used as in Standard English. The Future Tense of 'can' is 'will be able' as in:

'I'll be able to go tomorrow', the negative form of which is:

'I won't be able to go tomorrow.'

In Orkney dialect the negative form is expressed in two ways:

Ah'll no be able tae go the morn or:

Ah'll no can tae go the morn. This is a common and very interesting usage.

'Would' takes the forms *wid/wad* and are used in Orkney dialect exactly as in Standard English. Here are examples:

'I should begin'. 'I would rather . . .' . 'I might play'. 'I can go'. 'I could push'.

The negative forms of these verbs in English are 'shouldn't', 'wouldn't', 'mightn't', 'can't', 'couldn't'.

In Orkney dialect these take the form *shouldna/widna, mightna, canna, couldna*. Here are examples:

I shouldna provok him any more.

I widna go if I wir you.

I mightna go the morn.

I couldna see a thing wantan me glesses.

I canna wirk wi this bad hand.

The *na* suffix of the verb becomes 'not' if emphasis is required.

In Orkney dialect the expression *I widna say* is used in the sense 'I agree'. A Standard English exchange between two speakers for example might take this form:

Speaker: The weather's too rough for the boat to go today.

Listener: I agree.

A similar exchange between two Orkney dialect speakers would take the form:

Speaker: *The wather's too coorse fur the bot tae go the day.*

Listener: *I widna say.*

Compare remarks relating to *tae doot* on p. 57.

Subjunctive Tense

This tense is frequently used in foreign languages but is rare in English. Here is an example of the use of the Present Subjunctive in English:

'If you <u>be</u> good, I shall give you a sweet'. We would not expect to find the infinitive form of the verb '(to) be' here, rather we would expect the sentence to read:

'If you are good, I shall give you a sweet' and in fact that is the normal usage today since the Subjunctive Tense is gradually dying out in English. Formerly it was used wherever there was a degree of uncertainty about some future event, especially in cases where sentences began with 'if'. In Standard English the 'be' form is used throughout the Present Subjunctive:

I be	we be
you (singular) be	you (plural) be
he/she/it be	they be

Here is another example from English:

'If need <u>be</u> I'll have to go tomorrow'. This sentence means, 'If there <u>is</u> need . . .'

The reader will be delighted to learn that the Subjunctive is rarely used in the dialect of Orkney today—but it was used by older people. Here is an illustration of usage which may be found in old dialect writing:

If thoo <u>bees</u> good Ah'll gae thee a sweetie.

Notice that the Present Subjunctive of Orkney dialect

differed from Present Subjunctive of Standard English 'to be' in the use of *bees* instead of 'be'! In this instance *bees* is a short form of obsolete English 'beest', i.e. 'be-est'.

Today people who use the *thoo* form would generally say:

If thoor good Ah'll gae thee a sweetie.

Old people also used the word *beeswill* frequently as in this instance:

Beeswill we'll git tae the paet hill the morn.

The use of *bees* here is an extremely archaic form of English which still existed on the Scottish mainland up until the 17th century when a phrase such as 'Gif neid beis', i.e. 'If need be' could be heard.

Beeswill is a contracted form of '*Bees hid His will*' which in English is 'If it be His (i.e. God's) will'. The sentence above therefore reads:

'God willing, we'll get to the peat hill tomorrow'.

The Subjunctive is also used in English after 'as if' as in: 'He looked at me as if I were a fool.' The normal form of the verb would be 'I was' and we frequently hear this spoken today since the Subjunctive is dying out. In Orkney dialect, the phrase *sam as* is frequently used for 'as if', as in this example: *He lukkèd at me sam as I wir a fool.* The reader will realise that *wir* in this dialect example is the normal form of the verb and not the subjunctive.

The Pronunciation of Orkney Dialect[*]

The point was made earlier that dialect is constantly changing. If we go back five hundred years, what kind of dialect did the common man in Orkney speak? At that time it would have been a mixture of the Old Norse language and Scots and we get a good idea of this language from the Lord's Prayer, recorded in Orkney and Shetland at the end of the 18th century. Since prayers are very resistant to change we can safely assume that such prayers would be reasonably representative of the prayers spoken in chapels throughout the islands at the end of the 15th century. Here is the Lord's Prayer as it would have been spoken in Orkney about five hundred years ago:

Favor i – ir i Chimerie
Helleut var Nam thite
Gilla kongdum thine cumma
Veya thine mota, var gort o Yurn, finna gort in Chimeri
Gav us da dagloght brow vora
Firgive vuss sinna vora
Fin vee firgive sindara muth vus
Lyv vus ye i tumtation
Min delivra vus fro olt ilt.

The reader can see how Norse words such as *Chimerie* for 'heaven' (a corruption of *himin-ríki*) and *Yurn* (a corruption of *jorð-in*) give way later to English words such as 'forgive', 'temptation', 'deliver' and so on.

Let me move on to a time when our dialect becomes a little

---

[*] the whole of this chapter is spoken in dialect (with some slight modifications) on the accompanying CD.

bit more understandable. Without doubt our greatest dialect writer was Walter Traill Dennison who wrote in the 19th century dialect of the island of Sanday. I could include some of his writing but since it is the dialect of the West Mainland which is discussed in the book, I shall choose a dialect writer who is not so well known.

In 1931 J. T. Smith Leask, a Stenness man, wrote a book entitled *Peculiar People and Other Orkney Tales.* In it he included some fine stories which he tried to write in the dialect of old folk who lived around the year 1900. Anyone in his eighties living in 1900 would have learned the dialect about 1830 and so the stories recounted by Leask represent how a Stenness man would have spoken dialect over a hundred and seventy years ago. In the story I have chosen, Leask tells how Harry Clouston from Upper Cumminess in Stenness coped when, during the Napoleonic War, he was set upon by members of the Press Gang who tried to take him for the King's Navy. Some Orcadians even may find this short story difficult to understand and so here is a short outline by way of preparation.

Harry (or 'Herry' as Leask called him) was coming home from the peat hill one night with his peat cutting tool under his arm when the Press Gang constables jumped out of the heather and grabbed him. He lashed out with the peat cutter, ran for home, bolted the door, had a quick drink of buttermilk, took out of the fire a peat with a red hot end and when one of the constables tried to force the door, Harry stuck the red hot peat in his face. This is Leask's version:

> *Ae een, i da grimleens, Herrie wass haddan*
> *fur hame fae da hill wi is tuskar anunder 'is oxter*
> *an 'is hans i 'is bickets. He'd been gae-an some*
> *puir bothy a day's paet shaeran - mibbee ane he*
> *wass behadden tae, wha kens. Da Press Gang met*

im bit whin dey made tae lay hans apin im - e
yeused da tusker wi aa is birr api dem - an keepid
da hale swad at erms lent - fill he wan hame
pooran o swaet. E gid ane ur twa a good cloor.
Whin he wan in - da door wass made fest, an
Ah'm sheur du wadna giss i aa dee days - whitna
droll wappan wass prepared. E wass fairly fantan,
sae while he gleupid a sap o loots an bursteen, a
muckle paet wass pittan api da fire - fill ids
boddam wass rade haet an dan whin any o da
gang shaa'd is face, Herrie, fairly yiver, dabbid
da haet paet apin hid. Trath beuy, sheu wass a
coorse wappan, bit haith, sheu deud fine, sheu
raffled dem!

Notice the biggest change from the dialect of today. Leask speaks of *da hill*, *da door*, *da fire*, *da haet paet* instead of 'the hill', 'the door', 'the fire', 'the haet paet'. 'Thee' is pronounced *dee*, 'they' is pronounced *dey*, and 'them' as *dem*. All initial 'th' sounds are pronounced with a 'd'; Shetlanders still do this today but this pronunciation is completely lost in Orkney though an old story from Harray still records its use. Two old ladies were arguing about who owned a pigeon and one challenged the other by saying, *Dat's no dee doo Dora, dee doo deed* - 'That's not your pigeon Dora - your pigeon died'! There are some other unfamiliar pronunciations such as *puir bothy* for 'poor buddy'.

Leask began his tale with the words *ae een* meaning 'one evening'. 'One' used to be pronounced 'ae' in the olden days and when I was collecting Orkney words and expressions in the 1980s a Stenness resident told me that he had heard about a lady who was going to knit a jersey in 'a ae oo', meaning 'all wan wool (colour)'! Notice that 'home' in the passage is pronounced 'hame', another common Shetland pronunciation today. Leask says that Harry Clouston *keepid the hale <u>swad</u>* o constables at arm's length. This word *swad* represents the English word 'squad' but the Orcadian at that time pronounced a 'qu' as 'wh'. The English word 'queen' for example was pronounced 'wheen'. When Prince George visited Orkney in 1920 he was introduced to an old man who asked him, *Hoo's thee mither, the wheen keepan?* It's hardly a question to ask of a member of the Royal Family! It is still possible to hear 'qu' pronounced as 'wh' today e.g. when someone says 'white it!' for 'quit it' and the farm name 'quoy' can be pronounced 'why' or 'whee'. As an example, the farm house of Leaquoy in Marwick is locally pronounced *Leugh-whee*. An old form of pronunciation which cannot be shown from the chosen story is the pronunciation of 'th' as in 'thing'. It may still be heard today when someone addresses a child as a 'bit-a-ting'. The farm of Tingwall in Rendall originally would have been sounded *Thingvöllr* because that is where the 'thing' or parliament met in Norse times. One can still hear old folk count *ane, twa, tree* and use the word *twa-tree* meaning 'two or three'. The word 'thumb' was always pronounced *toom* and when butter used to be spread on bread with the thumb it was called 'toomspread'.

Apart from pronunciation in this excerpt, there are some good dialect words here too such as *grimleens* for 'dusk'; *tuskar,* an implement for cutting peat; *oxter* the armpit; *birr* force; *cloor* a swipe; *gleupid* gulped; and *yiver* energetic. As for the words *bursteen* and *loots*, they were the staple diet of Orkney folk at that time. For Orcadian ears nowadays there are two very unusual words in that passage. The most unusual word in the whole story is *fill*. It is used twice for example in this sense, *he pat a paet on the fire fill hids boddam wis red haet. Fill* is the old Scots pronunciation of 'while' but it is used here in the sense of 'until'. The other unusual word used is *wan* as a verb. It was said for example that Harry Clouston *<u>wan</u>* hame and *he <u>wan</u>* in. This word has nothing to do with the English word 'went'. It is the English verb 'to win' but used in the sense 'to go'. This usage is still known in Orkney. My Birsay neighbour told me that he *couldna win in* when something fell down behind the door and jammed it.

We have given an example of Orkney dialect as it was spoken over a hundred and seventy years ago. Now let us turn to the dialect spoken in the West Mainland of Orkney at the beginning of the 21st century. Here is the story of Little Red Riding Hood, told for the first time in Orkney dialect:

> *Wance thir wir a fine peedie lass thit*
> *everybody loved bit nobody loved har more ur har*
> *grandmither. The grandmither wir aalwis tryan*
> *tae think o new praesents tae gae the peedie lass.*
> *Wance sheu gid har a bonnie peedie red velvet*
> *hood an becaes the peedie lass suited hid so weel*
> *an never wanted tae wear anything ither,*
> *everybody jist caa'd har Peedie Red Riding Hood.*
> *Wan day har mother said tae har, 'Come thee wiz*
> *Peedie Red Riding Hood - here's a piece o kek an*
> *a bottle o wine noo; tak them ower tae thee*
> *grandmither wid thoo fur sheu's no feelan aal that*
> *weel an kinda wek. Sheu'll fairly enchoy them*
> *Ah'm sure. Anywey, awey thoo goes afore hid gits*
> *too hot noo and lik a good peedie lass waatch*
> *theesel in that forest. Fur mercy sek mind and no*
> *laeve the path ur yi'll mibbee faa and brak the*
> *bottle an than yir granny'll git notheen. Whin yi*
> *git there jist lift the snek and go in.*
>
> *'Ah'll waatch mesel mammy,' Peedie Red*
> *Riding Hood said tae har mither and aff sheu gid.*

This story shows some of the main differences between Orkney dialect and Standard English. I began by saying *wance thir wir* a peedie lass. This is very common in dialect. We say for example *I wir there yaesterday* and *He wir there too*—using *wir* instead of *wis*.

Whereas the English translation of the fairy tale describes Red Riding Hood as a 'sweet little girl', the Orkney translation is a 'fine peedie lass'. The word *peedie* is very commonly applied to children. When Stenness School was a two roomed school, one room was called the 'big end' and the other the *peedie* end. Both rooms were the same size but the reference was to the size of the children in it and not to the size of the rooms! *Peedie* is used too for anything small such as a *peedie finger* or a *peedie gren o sugar* and if anything is very small we say it is *peedie-oddy*. *Peedie breeks* is a favourite word to use for a child!

The English translation of the fairy tale says that the hood which Red Riding Hood wore 'suited her' but Orkney folk would say that 'sheu suited the hood'. This is an example of the many English expressions in Orkney dialect which we express in a back to front fashion. Here are some more—*ootside-in* for 'inside-out', *needles and preens* for 'pins and needles', *netting wire* for 'wire netting' and *sole stockeens* for 'stocking soles'— the list is endless and I have no explanation why Orkney folk do this!

Turning to another point in the Orkney version of the fairy tale, the mother said that granny would fairly *enchoy* the cake and wine. Orcadians have great difficulty pronouncing some letters, in this case, the letter 'j'. In the alphabet it is pronounced 'chy' and when it appears in a word it is sounded as if it were 'ch'. The letter 'g' is pronounced 'chee' in the alphabet and the soft 'g' as in words such as 'generally' and 'gin' are pronounced 'ch'. There is no distinction in Orkney dialect between 'gin' and 'chin'! The letter 'h' is pronounced 'itch' and, unlike many dialects of English, this letter is always sounded at the beginning of a word. There appears to be one exception when 'hospital' is sounded *ospital* but this is in fact the old Scots written form of the word which is still retained in dialect speech.The letter 'y' is never sounded in the word 'year'. This can probably be explained by our connection with the Old Norse language which, alone among the Germanic languages, also lost the initial consonant and developed the form *ár* for 'year'. As for the letter 'z' in the alphabet it is pronounced 'sed' and when it is the first letter in a word it is sounded the same as the letter 's'. A Standard English speaker would see a 'zebra in a zoo' but an Orcadian would see a *sebra in a soo*.

I should like to draw the reader's attention to a piece of advice that Red Riding Hood's mother gave her when she said *Watch theesel noo* where an English speaker would say 'Take care now'. *Watch theesel noo* is a common piece of advice given to young and old alike and *Watch theesel* is a common farewell greeting too. *Watch and no* means 'take care that you don't'. For example, an Orkney electrician, speaking dialect, might say, *Watch an no trip ower that cable noo*. A English workman would give the advice, 'Mind you don't trip over that cable now.' And so we leave Red Riding Hood to look at our dialect in a more particular way.

Thirty years ago—and almost to the day—I wrote an article for *The Orcadian* newspaper on Orkney dialect. Some may remember this article. I entitled it 'We call a spade a spade'. In that article I was not concerned so much about the words we use but our pronunciation. We all speak English of a kind although some foreigners on hearing our dialect for the first time might disagree. Here is an instance of that. When a Norwegian fishing boat anchored off Wyre a local man thought that he would row out and speak to someone on board. By good luck he could see a Norwegian on deck. The lone rower came alongside and shouted, *Does thoo spaek Eengleesh?* 'Yes', the man replied, 'but you don't.'

The Scots call our dialect Insular Scots—the Scots language spoken on the islands but that is not a very good description. It seems to suggest that there would not be very much difference between the speech of a Papay man and someone from the island of Arran. Along with the Shetland dialect it should be called Norn Scots.

Every Orcadian speaks two languages in fact—there is the language used in the family or among Orkney folk we know well—then there is the other language we use when we are among strangers or when we speak to someone in authority. In this latter instance we talk of *spaekan proper*. *Spaekan proper* really means trying to speak the very best English we can and it isn't easy! Ever since I started school and learned from my teachers to *spaek proper* I have been trying my best to master the English language. I think I can write correct English and, when the occasion requires it, I can speak Standard English but I'm still not good enough. Now and then there is always someone who will say to me, 'I can't place that accent,' or, more frequently, 'Are you Welsh?' On one occasion a Welshman asked me, 'What part of Wales do you come from?' I have never been taken for a Scotsman!

How is it that, after so many years of practice and using all the correct words, I cannot still speak English no matter how hard I try? The answer lies in the way we speak English—the intonation or song of the dialect. Every dialect of English has a song; even the Standard English speaker from the Home Counties has a song. Let us suppose that a new neighbour who came from Buckingham spoke to a Mrs. Clouston over the garden wall saying, 'How are you today Mrs. Clouston?' and Mrs Clouston answered *No so bad ither, thank you*. The neighbour would begin on a high note, his voice dropping down and levelling off. As for Mrs Clouston herself, her voice jumps up and down the scale and ends on a high note. Orcadians have a very distinct lilt to their voice. It goes up and down the whole time. Scots do not have this lilt but they do have a song too of a kind. Let us take the English sentence, 'I hope we can eat at eight o clock,' and compare two Scots, one from Glasgow and one from Fife speaking that sentence. The Glaswegian would start on as high note, go even higher, go very low then thump out the last word. As for the Fifer, he would start on a high note, sing a little song in the middle and do a little trill on the word 'clock'. Contrast that with the Orcadian whose voice swings up and down as he utters the sentence.

Where does this lilt in our voice come from? Does it come from our Scandinavian connection? In Norwegian, the sentence 'I hope we can eat at eight o clock is *Jeg håper vi kann spise klokken åtte* and it would be sounded with a similar lilt, going up and down just as in the Orkney dialect. Though Orcadians have a lilt like Norwegians, the Shetland dialect has no lilt at all. From where did our lilt come? A Dutch researcher has recently suggested that our dialect has a lilt because, unlike the Shetlanders, we live near folk who speak Gaelic! The truth is that Orcadians have had little contact with the Gaelic speakers of Sutherland. I would suggest that Orcadians do in fact have the Norse lilt and that Shetlanders have completely lost it and speak far more like the Scots. In fact that same piece of Dutch research showed that when the words of sentences are removed electronically and just the sounds are left, Shetlanders could not distinguish between their own dialect and an Edinburgh accent though Orcadians had no trouble at all! The answer to the question I posed at the beginning, 'How is it that, after so many years of practice and using all the correct words, I cannot still speak English?'—is that it is very difficult to git rid of the song of the dialect once it has been learned.

So much for our dialect intonation; apart from the intonation, there are many other differences such as those we noticed in my reading of the fairy tale—the words we use, how we express the vowels *a, e, i, o, u* and the consonants that go to make up all the other letters in the alphabet.

Both the word 'vowel' and the word 'consonant' mean merely 'sound'. The main difference between them is that in the vowels 'a', 'e', 'i', 'o' and 'u', the sound that comes out of the mouth is not blocked in any way but in the consonants the sound is blocked as it passes through the mouth, either by the tongue or the lips. In the case of the consonants 'm' and 'n', when the sound is blocked, it escapes through the nose. If we have a bad cold and the nose is blocked it becomes very difficult to pronounce 'm' and 'n'. There used to be a joke in our family about a lady with a very bad head cold who had tea with us. My mother had just made some plum jam and when the lady saw it on the table she said, *My I deu like plub jab.*

Let's look at the consonants first of all for they are the easier to study. We have said a little about them already in the Red Riding Hood passage. Older folk may still be heard pronouncing the *g* and *k* in a very interesting way. The hard *g* was pronounced as if it were 'dee' followed by a 'y'. 'Close the gate' would be sounded as *Close the dee-yet.* The many *geos* or inlets in the Birsay coast are locally called *dee-yoes.* An elderly person may still address one in these words *Whar are thoo dee-yan the day?*, 'Where are you going today?' Many of our place-names end in *gar* or *garth,* meaning 'farm'. This 'g' is very often pronounced as a 'dee-y' too. By far the best example is the old farm in Stenness which should be written 'Brogar'. In an attempt to record the local pronunciation, the Ordnance Survey put a 'd' in the word as well as a 'g' which make those who do not know better to pronounce the name 'Brodgar' which is completely wrong. The farm of Smoogarth in Firth is locally pronounced *Smodyar* but no 'd' is entered in the spelling of this name!

The letter 'k' may frequently be heard pronounced 'tee-y'. 'You'll know my husband well' will sound in dialect, *Thoo'll tee-yen me man weel*. 'Put on the kettle and we'll have a cup of tea' is *Pit on the tee-yettle and we'll hiv a cup o tea*.

In Standard English a 't' followed by 'h' is pronounced in two different ways. The pronunciation of 'thistle' and 'this' illustrates this difference. Some elderly folk pronounce the 'th' of 'thistle' as a simple 't' and so when a child gets a thistle in his thumb, granny may say *bit a ting—thoor gotten a tistle in thee toom*. Great granny in her time would have said *bit a ting—<u>dooer</u> gotten a tistle in <u>dee</u> toom!* It's still possible to hear these words spoken in Shetland. In Standard English the 'g' in 'ng' is sometimes pronounced with a hard sound and sometimes not. Orcadians share some of these different pronunciations with Standard English but in other cases there is a difference. As in English we do not pronounce the 'g' in 'singer'. In Standard English the 'g' in 'finger' is pronounced but in the dialect of Orkney 'singer' and 'finger' rhyme!

The way in which a consonant is pronounced depends very much on what comes before it and what comes behind it. The letter 'b' or 'd' in front of 'l' is very often missed out in dialect. We say *thimmle* and *rummle* for 'thimble' and 'rumble'. There are one or two Rummly Geos along the Orkney coastline where the sea makes a *rumlan* noise as it washes the boulders to and fro. As far as the letter 'd' in front of 'l' is concerned, Orkney brooms have *hanles* and not 'handles' and when there is a power cut and all the lights go out Orcadians look for *canles*. So much for 'd' in front of 'l'; if 'l' comes in front of 'd' on the other hand, 'd' is missed out! It is easy to show this with personal names. Harald is pronounced 'Haral', Donald is 'Donal' and Ronald, 'Ronal'. In place-names too we say North and South *Ronalsay*— there is no 'd' sound at all in these examples. Another thing to notice about the pronunciation of the place-name 'Ronaldsay' is that in Orkney dialect it is frequently sounded *Ronalshay*. The 's' is pronounced as if it were 'sh'. The reason for this is that 's' after 'd' changes the 's' to a 'sh' sound. In old maps we can actually find Ronaldsay written 'Ronaldshay'. The letter 'r' before 's' has the same effect on the pronunciation of the 's'. 'Birsay' is pronounced locally as if it were 'Birshee'. Should one wish to establish whether or not someone has a good Orcadian accent one must ask him or her to pronounce 'Birsay'—it is very difficult for non Orcadians to express the unique 'sh' sound in that place-name. Likewise it is very difficult for an Orcadian to say in Standard English 'cars' or 'bars' and 'purser's' as in 'purser's office' is almost impossible to say!

The consonants as we have seen are reasonably easy to discuss. Vowels, on the other hand, present us with many difficulties—even in Standard English where, although we have only five vowels, they are used to represent at the very least thirteen vowel sounds—and when we come to Orkney dialect, even more! There is a further complication. We noted that when two consonants come together as in the case of 'r' and 's' above we get a completely different sound for the *s*. Where two vowel sounds come together, exactly the same thing happens. In Standard English, p-e-t is 'pet' and p-a-t is 'pat' but p-ea-t is 'peat'. This does not happen in every language. In the Italian language for instance, every vowel must be pronounced separately. When two vowel sounds are pronounced together in English to make another sound we call it a 'diphthong'. 'Diphthong' means merely 'two sounds'.

Along with the 'song' of the dialect which has already been discussed, the vowels and the diphthongs make a big contribution to the uniqueness of Orkney dialect. When I translated the passage of Red Riding Hood into Orkney dialect, I had to change 37% of all the vowel sounds. Here are just a few chosen at random:

once	*wance*
grandmother	*grandmither*
because	*becaes*
suited	*sooted*
cake	*kek*
weak	*wek*
break	*brak*
nothing	*notheen*

There are absolutely no hard and fast rules for the pronunciation of vowel sounds in Orkney dialect—they just have to be learned! The same is true of Standard English of course. Take the word 'bowl' in English. Orcadians pronounce it *bowl* to rhyme with 'owl'. In English four hundred years ago this word was spelt 'bolle' but it was pronounced 'bowl' (to rhyme with 'owl'). English script writers thought that there should be a 'w' in it to indicate the pronunciation and so it came to be spelt 'bowl'. Unfortunately the <u>pronunciation</u> in England later changed to 'boll' but the spelling with the 'w' remained! In Orkney we are stuck with the original pronunciation *bowl* (rhyming with 'owl') which sounds very strange to English ears today!

The difficulty of writing anything about the pronunciation of vowels can be shown by looking at the English word 'done'. Although the first vowel in that word is 'o' the word is pronounced 'dun' but what about the pronunciation in Orkney dialect? Here is a snippet of conversation at the end of a meal in an Orkney house:

Hostess: *Are thoo deun wi thee tea?*

Guest : *Yaas, Ah'm doan - thank you.* In dialect we have two different ways of pronouncing 'done' and neither is like the Standard English form!

Let us look at the vowel sounds generally to see whether we can make some helpful generalisations. We'll begin with the sounds represented by the letter 'a' in the alphabet.

In Standard English 'a' has a short sound as in 'arm'. In dialect, many short sounds are pronounced differently from Standard English. English 'arm' becomes *erm* in dialect; English 'apple' is *epple* and English 'sack', *sek*.

The long 'a' sound as in 'cake', 'bake' and 'sake' is pronounced as if it were a short 'e'. In Orkney dialect these words would be sounded *kek, bek* and *sek*. The long 'a' in words like 'late', 'rate' and 'date' however are sounded as if they were the 'i' in English 'it'. 'Late', 'rate' and 'date' change to *laet, raet* and *daet*.

Now we turn to the short 'e' as in 'bed' or 'well' where 'well' means 'healthy'. 'Bed' is pronounced 'bayd' and 'well' meaning 'healthy' is *weel*. Where 'well' carries the meaning 'well of water' however it is pronounced *waal*. This vowel sound 'aa' in 'waal' which is quite rare in dialect is peculiar to Orkney as far as I can make out. In Firth, Rendall, Evie and Rousay this vowel may be heard in the pronunciation of English 'all'. In those parishes the sentence 'It's alright to take it all,' would be spoken *Hid's aal right tae tak hid aal.*

The long 'e' in English in words like 'peat', 'heat' and 'meat' where 'meat' in this sense is 'flesh' are sounded *paet, haet* and *maet* but the long 'e' in 'meet', 'beet' and 'feet' are sounded exactly as in English!

The Standard English short 'i' is pronounced in two ways in Orkney dialect. 'Sit down for a little bit' would be sounded *Sit doon for a peedie bit* but with a far more open 'i' sound. This is the same open 'i' which is heard in the dialect pronunciation of 'fish'. In other instances 'i' is pronounced as if it were a long 'e'! A 'wicked king' is a *weekid keeng*. 'Kick' is *keek*, 'sick' is *seek* and 'quick' is *queek* but there is no hard and fast rule since 'lick' is *lick* and 'thick' is *thick*!

The vowel 'u' may be pronounced in three ways in English. The three separate words 'fur', 'fury' and 'full ' in the sense of 'filled up' bring out these three differences in pronunciation. As in English we use the first two vowel sounds but 'full' in dialect is pronounced to rhyme with English 'dull'. The words 'bull' and 'pull' also rhyme with English 'dull'.

There are two vowel sounds in Orkney dialect which have no counterpart in English. Here are examples of the first. One may frequently hear a 'duck' referred to as a *deuk* and a hook as a *heuk*. When I decided to go on to school and not go out to work like the rest of the family, my granny thought I was a shirker but she didn't call me that, she called me a *fleunk*. The second unusual vowel sound exists in only one word frequently used in Orkney dialect today and that is in the word *beuy,* a form of English 'boy'. *Beuy* is used only in forms of address such as the common greeting *Aye beuy* when it has a friendly ring about it but in a command such as *Come here beuy!* it is rather offensive. These vowel sounds cannot be demonstrated without recourse to a phonetic alphabet but they are easily understood from the accompanying CD.

There are many differences between Orkney dialect and Standard English when we consider the diphthongs. Nearly all 'aw' sounds in English such as 'awful', 'paw', 'raw', 'saw', 'straw' and so on are pronounced 'aa'. Translate them into Orkney dialect and we have *aafil, paa, raa, saa* and *straa*. This extended 'a' is unknown in English. In some places in Orkney 'straw' is pronounced 'stray'. The old story is told about a farmer who placed a notice in *The Orcadian* newspaper to say that 'all stray dogs coming on my land will be shot' and, as a prank someone pulled his leg by making a dog out of straw and placing it in the farm yard!

The double 'o' diphthong in English may be pronounced in two different ways in Standard English as in 'food' and 'root'. Orcadian dialect does not have the long 'oo' sound as in 'food'. 'Food' in dialect is pronounced with the short sound, just as it is in English 'root'. It is still very common to hear other ways of sounding the double 'o' in dialect. Dialect pronunciation of the following sentences may be heard on the accompanying CD:

1. *We hiv tae pull aal weeds oot bi the reut.*
2. *In weet wather we hiv tae wear rubber beuts.*
3. *Hid's a right bonny meun the night.*

Lastly we turn our attention to the diphthong 'ow' generally represented by the letters 'ou' or 'ow' together as in words such as 'sound', 'loud', 'mouth' and so on. In dialect, these words are pronounced *soond*, *lood*, and *mooth*. Unfortunately there are many exceptions to this rule. Orkney has plenty of Neolithic mounds and they are all called 'mounds' as in English. However, although a 'pound' in money is pronounced 'pound' a pound weight is pronounced *pund*. In a shop today a good piece of cheese may cost as much as four *pound a pund*.

And so we end our review of the pronunciation of Orkney dialect. I began by reading the Lord's Prayer as it would have been spoken in Orkney five hundred years ago. I thought it would be a fitting conclusion to write the Lord's Prayer in the dialect spoken today:

> *Wir faither*
> *Thit's in heaven*
> *Hallowed be thee name*
> *Thee keengdom come*
> *Thee will be done—*
> *On earth sam as hid is in heaven*
> *Gae hiss the day wir daily bread*
> *And forgive hiss wir trespasses—*
> *Sam as we forgive them thit trespass against hiss*
> *And don't laed 'iss intae temptation*
> *Bit deliver 'iss fae evil*
> *Fur thine is the keengdom*
> *The power and the glory*
> *Fur ivver and ivver. Amen*

So yir been strugglan wi the pronunciation o Orkney dialect?
Here is a light-herted guide tae the pronunciation, based on the
anonymous English poem thit follows.

Pronunciation fur Ferryloupers

I tak hid yi already ken
Thit keetcheen's but bit bedroom's ben
Ither fok—bit niver you
Will mispronounce alloo and broo.
Weel done! Noo doon below yi'll see a few
Thit yi should try and wirk on noo.
Waatch oot fur owld instead o old
Hid's aalwis cowld hid's niver cold.
Weak is wek and sack is sek
Take is tak and bake is bek
Instead o went yi must say gid
We don't say wood hid's aalwis wid
A Orkney man'll mow the laan
And when he's tired he'll likly yaan
Orkney cats are fond o craem
And sleepan dogs'll affens draem
Whin wir seek and canna aet
Wir niver ill, wir aff the baet
We don't say mess, hid's aalwis maes
And whin we die we rest in paes.
Yi think yi'll niver mind hid oan—
Words like aal and claes and doan
Hiss fur us and wir fur our?—
I kent hid aal whin I wir fower!

Gregor Lamb

So you have been struggling with the pronunciation of Orkney dialect? Then spare a thought for all foreigners who have to cope with the notoriously difficult pronunciation of English!

Pronunciation for Foreigners

I take it you already know
Of tough and bough and cough and dough?
Others may stumble, but not you,
On hiccough, thorough, lough and through.
Well done! And now you wish perhaps
To learn of less familiar traps?
Beware of heard, a dreadful word,
That looks like beard and sounds like bird.
And dead: it's said like 'bed', not 'bead'—
For goodness sake don't call it 'deed'!
Watch out for meat and great and threat
(They rhyme with suite and straight and debt).
A moth is not a moth in mother
Nor both in bother, broth in brother.
And here is not a match for there,
Nor dear and fear for bear and pear,
And then there's dose and rose and lose—
Just look them up—and goose and choose,
And cork and work and card and ward.
And font and front and word and sword,
And do and go and thwart and cart—
Come, come, I've hardly made a start!
A dreadful language? Man alive!
I'd mastered it when I was five!

Anon

Dialect Writing

Orkney fok are gret fur yarnan. This story is based on a tale I hard in Orkney in the 1980s.

The Kep

He niver hard me coman in fur he wis gittan kinda daef.

'Whit like the day than?' I asked.

Robbie turned roond aakwardly in his chair and lukkèd ower his glesses, 'Good hid's thee, I niver hard thee min. I don't like this fok gan roond wi rubber soled shoes, hid's liken tae fleg owld fok like mesel.'

'I wisna tryan tae fleg yi!'

'I ken that owerweel bit when yi git tae me age and yir sittan readan the paeper and aal o a sudden thir's a voice, my hid does gae a buddy a gluff. Sit doon min.'

Robbie pits the paper doon and the cat sittan on his shoolder hads on fur grim daeth as he leans forward tae gae the fire a pok. The claas dig through his shirt intae the skin.

'An a doreen on thee, cat. Tak the cat aff me shoolder min wad thoo. Hid's in a ferfil aakward piece fur me tae git had o hid.'

I oblige.

'Weel whit's deuan?'

'I hiv a story fur thee the day.'

'Whit's that than?'

Robbie stands ap, taks his pipe and baccy aff the mantelpiece, sits doon and begins tae stap the bowl fill o a Warlock mixter.

'Beuy Ah'm hin a most ferfil interestan visitor the day,' he stricks a match bit hid braks.

'Ferfil trowie matches nooadays min,' he stricks again and thir's a lowe. He sooks and sooks again and a comfortan wisp o blue reek drifts ap fae the bowl. He shaks the match, the flame goes oot and he haeves hid in the fire. He sits there puffan contentedly and Ah'm winderan if this story is iver gan tae stert.

'Whar wis yir visitor than?'

'A wife fae the sooth.'

'A bonny wife?'

'Feth a weel lukkan wife.'

'Did yi ken sheu wis coman?'

'Feenty bit o me. I wis in the oothoose whin I hard this car coman ap tae the door so oot I goes and this wife wir jumpan oot o hid. I thowt mibbe sheu wis askan fur directions bit na sheu kam right ap tae me and said, 'You must be Mr. Johnston,' an tuk me ferly bi surprise.

'I don't ken thee,' I said.

'No' sheu said, 'you won't but we do have a connection.'

My that did set me winderan. 'Whit's thee name?' I speered har.

'Felicity Hodge,' sheu said, 'bit that name won't mean anything to you. My maiden name was Louard.'

'Louard,' I said tae mesel, 'mercy Ah'm hard that name afore. Yir mither wadna been Edwina Louard wad she?'

'Edwina Louard—that's right!' sheu said and her face lit ap in such a bonny smile. Lovely teeth sheu hid beuy teu and right bonny fair hair jist glistenan in the sun.

'Come in lass,' I said. In sheu kam and sat doon in that very chair yir sittan in noo.'

'Hoo can I help thee?' I askèd.

'My mother died recently at the age of ninety-four and I was looking through some of her things.'

She pat her hand in her pooch and pulled oot a owld crushed ap envelope.

'Do you recognise that?' sheu askèd as sheu passed me sometheen hidden in her hand.

'God a loaveen!' I said as I lukkèd doon at this thing lyan in me liv, 'dae I no! Thoor knockèd me clean stupeed.'

I lukkèd at har.

'This is the note that you sent with it,' sheu said, passan me a peedie bit a broon paper—hid wada been white at wan time. Hid wis me writeen right enough.

'Tell me the story Mr. Johnston,' sheu said.

'Na thoo tell me thee story first,' I said and sheu did.

'Our family lived in a little village called Horley in Sussex. My father worked in London—in the City, every day leaving early in the morning by train and coming home late at night. He wasn't happy in his work. He wanted a more adventurous life but mother was very happy where she was and didn't want to move especially since I was barely out of my pram at the time. Well when the war started he was immediately called up into the Royal Navy. You see after he left University he missed the company of his friends and had joined the Royal Naval Reserve. After he married, my mother would not let him go to any more meetings but of course the Admiralty traced him. My mother was so upset when he had to go but it just gave Dad that thrill which he felt was missing from his life. He was immediately commissioned and rose through the ranks very quickly. He loved his uniform and mother told me that she loved to see him in his uniform too. Now you tell me what you can remember Mr. Johnston.'

'Weel I could see thit the wife wis nearaboot greetan so I thowt I wad tell har me side o the story.

'Hid's like this,' I said, 'I wirna in the war fur I hid tae bide home and wirk on the ferm. Anybody thit wrowt on a ferm could bide home yi see. Weel wan bonny Sunday morneen I tuk a waak doon tae the shore. A ferfil o things yeused tae come in wi

the tide thanadays—so many boats gan doon yi see. Many a
thing I fand. Weel that morning the sea wis jist like gless, lovely
an calm. In fact a buddy could harly believe thir wis a war on.
Yeusally yi could see a boat ur two on the horizon bit thir wirna
anything like that oot there that morning bit as I wis lukkan I
thowt I saa something floatan oot by. Hid wis too far oot fur me
tae git had o, bit the tide wis coman in and I thowt tae mesel if
I waited a blinkie the tide wad tak hid in—and feth hid did. Hid
wis a kep—I kent hid wis a Naval Officer's kep fur thir wir a lot
o Naval officers doon at Twatt at that time and feth they wad
sometimes come by the hoose fur eggs and the like. Weel I
pickèd ap the kep and I thowt, 'Mercy whit'll I deu wi this?'—
hid belongs tae somebody—mibbe somebody thit's no here any
longer. I windered tae me if thir wir a name inside hid fur I kent
thit they aalwis pat thir names inside and when I lukkèd, deed
thir wir a name. On a sma bit a white label inside there wir a
name thit I could harly read becaes the sea watter wir nearaboot
washed hid awey. Whin I got home I shaa'd hid tae the wife and
wi a magnifying gless we both made oot 'Felix Louard'. Bit
mercy whin we wir hivan a good luk at the kep, tuckèd right ap
in the peak thir wir a peedie brooch pinned in there. We tuk hid
oot and hid wis solid gold—as bright as the day hid wis made
and hid hid the name 'Edwina' on hid. Weel I thowt thit hid
might be possible tae return the kep tae the family so wan day
whin I wir gan doon tae Dounby I parcelled ap the kep and pat
a message inside wi me name and address. I gid ap the
Bryameadow road and thir wir a sentry on duty at the
aerodrome. I gid him the kep and the brooch and telt him whar
I fand hid and he said thit he wad pass hid on tae the Station
Commander and I niver hard tale o the kep ur the brooch again
till the day.'

Robbie got ap and tuk doon fae the mantelpiece a photo.
'Sheu left me that; sheu thowt I wad like hid,' he said.

Hid shaa'd a group o Naval Officers and a arrow in biro pen marked the most handsome o them aal.

I turned the picture ower. Written in pencil on the back wis:

Felix living it up in the Wardroom. HMS Hood, Scapa Flow, 1940

'Oh mercy, me pipe's gin oot,' said Robbie, 'wid thoo like a dram beuy?

'I widna say no,' I replied.

I wis very affens askèd bi Orkney folk tae write a piece o poetry fur them. In the 1980s the Orkney Goat Society askèd me if I wid mak a contribution tae thir magazine. I kent the man fine thit approached me. He wis President o the Orkney Goat Society, a Caithness man, a ferrylouper, thit hid come ower tae Orkney and married a local wife. I promised tae write something fur him and when I pat pen tae paeper I said tae mesel why no tak as me subject a Caithness billy goat coman ower tae Orkney and lukkan fur a nanny.

The Ferrylouper

A Caithness billy, feelan lonely,
Said he hid jist wan wish only
And that wish wis tae find a lass
Tae cook his dinner, mend and wash.
So he lukkèd high and low
Endan up at last in Thurso
Whar he met a passer by
Tae whar he asked the question why—
'Why is hid thit in this toon,
And fur many miles aroond,
In fact min—everywey Ah'm been,
Thir's no a nanny tae be seen?'
The passer by, he stops tae think
And than he gaes a knowan wink,
'Beuy if yi want a nanny goat
I suggest yi tak the Orkney boat—

Hunders o them there, hid's true,
Waitan fur a chap like you.
The day min is the best tae go
Fur hid's thir annual County Show.'
So doon he gid tae Scrabster pier
Tae find the fare wis kinda dear
Fur billies purest pedigreed—
Especially unaccompanied.
'If that's the caes, hid'll hiv tae be
Hid's aafil, this monopoly.'
Noo since his sea legs wirna good
He thowt hid better if he could
Pay the extree fur a berth
Tae speed the crossing o the Firth.
So straight awey he gid tae bed
And niver even raised his head
Fur the Pentland wis like gless
And soon the Ola roonded Ness.
The gang planked lowered—very soon
Wir Caithness billy's coman doon.
He speered a man than whar tae go
Tae catch a bus intae the Show.
Twa peedie boys began tae laugh
Bit billy fairly chaest them aff—
Than twa big splashes could yi hear—
He'd chaest them both right ower the pier!
The bus wis ready stannan there
He jumpèd in and asked the fare.
Tom Drever laughed—'Bit yir a goat—
Yi'll hiv tae find a cattle float!'
'Watch hid!' said wir Caithness billy
'Ah'm mibbe a goat bit no so silly
Don't come here wi any funny
Business—jist you tak me money.'

So that wis that—wi no more fuss
Tom Drever sterted ap his bus.
Noo on his journey tae the toon
Wir billy aalwis lukked aroond
He hoped thit soon his eye wid catch
A bonny nanny unattached.
Bit na, his luck seemed tae be oot,
Thir wisna wan at aal aboot—
Jist endless fields o boran kye
And fields o silage gress forbye.
'I hopp thit whit Ah'm done is right
Thir's no a single goat in sight!'
The bus stopped at the Bignold gate
And billy—he could harly wait
Tae git inside tae see the Show,
Oh beuy yi shoulda seen him go!
He hunted fur his entrance fee
Bit dae yi ken—he got in free.
He handed ower a crisp pound nott
Th'official said, 'Bit yir a goat—
Competitors don't hiv tae pey
So pit yir nott and purse awey.'
No sooner wis he in the yard
Than he wis certain thit he hard
A nanny caalan fae a pen,
He listened—than hid kam again
Than he belted doon the field so queek
He knocked a poor man aff his feet!
His brilliant dash paid dividends
Fur there, ahead o him wir pens
O gorgeous nannies, brilliant white,
He'd niver, iver, seen the like,
Wi mooths so sensuous, eyes so blue,
A fire burned inside him noo.

'Bit whit's this here? A special pen?'
He lukked at hid and lukked again,
Inside—a dream—a beauty there
Wi snow white face and finest hair.
'Please pardon me—are you the queen?
Fur yir the fairest thit Ah'm seen.'
She turned—and there, afore his eyes
Her rosette shaa'd sheu'd won first prize!
'Oh nanny, hear me story, please,
Fur you I go on bended knees,
Fur Ah'm been strivan aal me life
Tae find mesel a bonny wife.
Oh, can yi wash and cook and sew
And mak me happy whin Ah'm low?'
'Me mither said tae waatch the men—
Bit anything tae laeve this pen.'
'I winder noo if Ah'm in luck?
A final question—can yi butt?'
'Butt? I must be frank wi you
Yi'll hiv tae shaa me whit tae do.'
'Yi canna butt?! Weel I wis learned
Tae butt whin I wis jist a bairn!
Ah'll shaa yi an amazan scene
The finest butt yir ever seen!'
Wi no a little consternation
Sheu steud and waatched the demonstration.
He ran back aal o fifty yard
And at the pen he charged so hard
He knocked the pieces aal aboot
And knocked himsel completely oot!
She steud and stared fair mesmerised
And harly could believe har eyes.
'He caals hid *butt*—bit he means *doos*—
I think he'd no be muckle use.

I think Ah'm better aff withoot a chap
Thit uses funny words like that,
Fur whitna lass'll tak the hand
O a man sheu canna understand?'
She jumpèd through the broken pen
Tae luk fur ither likely men.
A blinkie laeter, slightly dazed,
He stirred and tae his feet he raised.
The pen wis empty, lover gone,
He thowt he'd better head fur home.
Withoot a doot, he wis concussed,
He'd better go and find the bus.
Than aff he gid, poor bit a thing
Bit wandered through the judgeen ring.
The chief judge jumpèd in the air,
'Jist luk whit's waakan ower there—
Oh aal the baest Ah'm iver seen
Oh champions, that wan is supreme.'
They aal agreed, no more wis said,
They fixed the ticket on his head.
So billy's trip, so nearly sad,
Ended ap no aal that bad,
The tributes, they kam in a flood
And billy ended ap at stud
And though he didna git a wife
He hid a middling dissent life!

Epilogue

If you are Orcadian and have reached the end, are you not pleased that you did not actively have to learn all this! If you are a 'sooth country buddy', good luck with your studies! You can test your fluency on P. 134.

Appendix I

Useful phrases to help you polish up your Orkney Dialect

a day atween weathers: a day of good weather between a series of days of bad weather.

aboot-gaan-buddy: someone who is always visiting.

abune a: unreasonable: *Bit no tae tell his mither he wis gittan married wis abune a.*

accorned tae the man: as it is said: *'Weel, accorned tae the man—hid'll git waar afore hid gits better.'*

aet afore a stone: better than no food at all: *An owld bere binnack'll aet afore a stone.*

aff the mind o: having had a change of mind: *We did want tae mov tae the toon bit wir aff the mind o'd noo.*

Ah'm hard the wind blowan afore: You (etc.) are unlikely to keep your promise.

best kens: I don't know.

best bliss thee: bless you.

bi time: early: *We'll hiv tae be up bi time the morn tae catch the boat.*

blisseens on thee: bless you.

(bonny) fine hid: I'm in agreement with your suggestion.

come against: having an abrasive personality: *He's an aafil come against man that.*

different wans: many people: *Different wans say thit he's no gan tae git married noo.*

far awey wi'd: eccentric in behaviour, usually associated with dotage.

had yir tongue: 1. be quiet! 2. a reaction to an unbelievable piece of news.

He's no hin a corn fork tae his erse: He's well bred.

hid'll be the day afore hid: an indication that something has to be postponed: *'I wis gan tae deu the washeen bit I doot hid'll be the day afore hid.'*

hingan taegither: in a very poor state of health.

hiv a keepeen on: to value something: *Thoo'll no can tae tak me gold brooch—I hiv a keepeen on hid.*

I hiv aal me back teeth up: I wasn't born yesterday.

in the hinder end: as a last resort. *In the hinder end we jist hid tae git a new back door.*

in all me born days: in aal my life: *Ah'm no seen such a raffle in aal me born days.*

lad o hid: *He's some lad o hid,* he's quite a character.

mak yir supper: an invitation to a guest to eat plenty at supper time: *Sit in noo and mak yir supper.*

mind and no: remember not to: *Mind an no go near the tractor noo.*

mixter o mercies: a variety of objects: *Thir's a mixter o mercies in this draaer.*

niver a bit o: certainly not: *Niver a bit o me's gan tae go:* i.e. I'm certainly not going.

niver spaek!: I completely agree: Speaker: *Whit a weet hid's been!* Listener: *Niver spaek!*

niver wis hid ither: things haven't changed. Speaker: *The money he earns on Thursday is spent bi Friday.* Listener: *Niver wis hid ither.*

no chaet fur: having plenty, but in a disparaging sense, usually with regard to personal appearance: *He's no chaet fur hair anywey.*

no in me minding: not that I can recall.

no can tae: to be unable to do something in the future: *He'll no can tae play golf noo thit he's dislocated his shoolder.*

none o the pair o them: neither.

noo and say: of uncertain outcome, usually of health: *Granny's no keeping that weel—she's jist noo and say.*

oot o the wey: only in the negative form *no oot o the wey*, not excessive: *Payan five pound fur that is no oot o the wey.*

oot-aboot: out and around: *Willie's gittan oot-aboot noo thit the days are on the turn.*

ootside in: inside out.

owerweel hid: That's fine by me!

owerweel kent: well known (only of something disparaging): *Hid's owerweel kent thit he's tarry fingered.*

sitten on: humiliated: *He wis right sitten on when he wisna made Chairman.*

tae come at: to improve in health: *He's been a poor buddy for long bit he's coman at noo.*

tae baet fleuks: to strike the arms across the chest to warms the hands.

tae be aback o: reluctant to: *She wisna aback o askan him.*

tae be in grand strip: revelling in a situation: *Owld Peter wis in grand strip at the waddeen last night—hid musta been the home brew!*

tae be upsides wi: having caught up with one's work: *Efter me bad back Ah'm jist aboot upsides wi the silage noo.*

tae chap and change: to be constantly changing something unnecessarily: *She's aalwis chappan and change-an her keetcheen.*

tae cheeter and laugh: to smirk, especially of children: *Stop that cheetereen and laugheen in the back o the car.*

tae doot: to be in agreement (only about a statement containing a negative idea): Speaker: *Wir seen the best of the day.* Listener: *I doot hid.*

tae fa sindry: to come to pieces by accident, age etc.

tae let on: only used negatively as in *Never let on*, keep it a secret.

tae mak drowth: to dry up, of the land etc.

tae mak weet: to rain.

tae mind on: to remember.

tae pit at: to annoy.

tae pit fur: to send for: *We hid tae pit fur the doctor last night.*

tae pit mad: to make angry.

tae redd ap kin: to discuss one's pedigree.

tae sit stridelegs: to sit astride.

tae the fore: of an elderly person, in good health: *Eddie is still tae the fore; I saa him on the tractor the tither day.*

tae wirk a wark: 1. to be busy 2. to play tricks 3. of an engine etc., to play up.

tae wirk the creels: to fish lobsters etc.

the height o hid: *That's aboot the height o hid*, a phrase used at the apparent conclusion of something e.g declaring to a shopkeeper that nothing more is needed.

the pair o them: both. *The pair o them is a disgrace tae the perrish.*

the rights o: usually in the phrase *tae hear the rights o* to know the exact details, usually of a rumour. *Thir wir this trouble in the street last night bit Ah'm niver hard the rights o hid.*

thir tellan me: it is said (that): *Thir tellan me thir's no gan tae be a boat the morn.*

this last peedie while: recently.

watch and no: mind that you don't: *Watch and no fa noo wi that high heels.*

weel amis: well deserved: *Hid wis weel amis that yi chappèd yir finger whin I telt yi no tae play wi'd.*

wi his braeth on his lip: in an excited state and out of breath: *He kam runnan ap the road wi his braeth on his lip sayan that a bale hid faan doon and hitten John.*

Appendix II

Sample of Words in Common Currency Drawn from *Orkney Wordbook*

Forms of Address

beuy: form of address to a male of any age: *Weel beuy, hoo are yi keepan?*
buddo: form of address to a child or an elderly lady: *Come noo buddo and hiv a bite o maet.*
lass: form of address to a woman of an age: *Weel lass, I niver saa yi lukkan so bonny.*
min: form of address to a man or boy: *Watch oot min—I widna trust that coo.*
umman: jocular form of address to a woman: *Come on umman—we'll be laet!*

Forms of Greeting

Aye: Hello: also frequently *Aye, aye.*
Whit like? How are you?
Whit wey are thoo? How are you?
Yaas: Hello; also frequently *Yaas, yaas.*

Adjectives

aff-takkan: disparaging: *He's aalwis makkan some aff-takkan remark aboot fok.*
bare naked: stark naked.
barkèd: of the skin, filthy dirty: *Go and wash yir hands beuy, thir jist barkèd.*
birny: of the weather, cold: *Hid's a cowld birny day the day.*
bowsie-leggèd/bowdy leggèd: bandy-legged.
breeksed: aching (after hard work): *Ah'm fairly breeksed efter me wark in the gairdeen this morneen.*
brimman: full to the brim.
burded: of an egg, having a chicken inside.
changey: changeable: *We don't ken whit tae mak o this wather—hid's ferfil changey.*
chirpan: soaking wet, especially of the feet: *My whit rain! Me feets jist chirpan.*
claggy: sticky.
cockly: liable to topple.
coorse: of the weather, rough: *Hid wir far too coorse fur the bairn tae go tae the school yesterday.*
deualess: lazy.

different: used in dialect in the phrase *different wans* with the meaning, 'a number of people': *Different wans are sayan thit the shop's gan tae close.*

faird: afraid: *He'll no go on the roof; he's faird he'll fa.*

fill: full or full up.

foggy: of a peat, turnip etc which has a loose granular structure.

foosty: smelling of mould.

gisless: showing little common sense.

godless: expressing extreme size, difficulty etc: especially in the phrase *most godless*: *Hid's a most godless size o a hoose thit he's biggan.*

goodly: church going: *She's a goodly buddy; she goes tae the kirk every Sunday.*

gushlan: clumsy.

gyte: crazy, especially in the phrase, *gan gyte*, 'going crazy'.

headlight: light-headed.

ill-nettered: awkward.

in-bund: confined e.g. of a house.

kittly: ticklish.

krom: hoarse.

lappered: of milk, sour.

lippan: of a bucket etc., full to the brim.

muckle: large.

murdered: bruised.

oot-feeted: splay footed.

ootside-in: inside-out.

owerweel: satisfactory, *Hid'll deu owerweel*, it is satisfactory.

parteeclar: 1. particular: *Ah'm no parteeclar whither I go or no.* 2. special in one way or another, especially in a reply: <u>Speaker</u>: *Grand day, min.* <u>Listener</u>: *Jist parteeclar.*

peedie: small.

peedie-oddie: very small.

rickly: of a structure, poorly built.

rory: of colours, bright, especially red.

sabbèd: soaking wet.

seekensome: (of food) sickening.

shoogly: unstable, of a chair etc.

shilpid: of a substance, sour: *My that plums is right shilpid.*

sirpan: soaking wet: *Whit a shooer o weet, Ah'm jist sirpan!*

skaoowaoo: squint: *That picture's aal skaoowaoo.*

skar: showing fear: *Me peedie cat's a ferfil skar thing.*

skeffly-feeted: clumsy.

slestry: wet, of weather etc.

smitsom: contagious.

smoored: in the phrase *smoored wi the cowld*, choked with a bad cold.

sooth: across the Pentland Firth, especially in the phrase *gan sooth*: *Ronnie says he's gan sooth wi the boat the morn.*

sooth country: anyone whose normal habitation is across the Pentland Firth: *Thir sayan thit sooth country fok's bowt Howan.*
spleet-new: brand new.
taldery: ragged.
thight: tight (Orcadians use the original English pronunciation!)
trowie: 1. of health, poor 2. of materials, poor quality.
trowie-like: unhealthy looking.
unfaandoon: in a state of imminent collapse.
unfaansindry: almost disintegrating.
unkan: unfamiliar, especially in the phrases *unkan fok (folk), unkan wife/man* etc.

Adverbs

a-pace: still, literally 'in peace': *Sit a-pace beuy and aet yir dinner.*
backleens: in a backwards direction.
backside foremost: the wrong way round: *Yir pittan that in backside foremost.*
erse-aboot-face: the wrong way round: *That bolt's gin in erse-aboot face.*
erseleens: with the backside first: *Try min and get through that peedie window erseleens.*
gey: very: *Hid's gey cowld the day.*
halfleens: half: *She wir halfleens oot o the window whin she got stuck!*
heels ower head: head over heels.
home-aboot: at home: *Is John home-aboot the day?*
in-aboot: inside (the house): *The bairns should bide in-aboot the day wi wather like this.*
kinda: rather: *Hid's kinda queer thit he gid aff withoot tellan iss.*
kindaweys: rather: *He's kindaweys like his faither.*
liken: likely: *He's liken tae cut himsel wi that sharp knife.*
naffil: expressing degree; *Thir hin a naffil wark wi thir dowter.*
nearaboot: almost: *He neeraboot got killed whin the scaffoldeen fell.*
normous: expressing degree: *Normous o kye forward the day at the mart min.*
oot-aboot: outside: *He can git oot-aboot noo thit the wather's a piece better.*
right: expressing degree: *Feth he's done right weel.*
sideyweys: in a sideways direction: *Pit hid in sideyweys, min.*
short ago: recently: *That canna be right—I saa him short ago.*
than: then: *I could ferly run than!*
waar: worse: *Hid's waar lukkan noo than hid wir afore.*
sindry: especially *tae tak sindry*, to take apart: *He'll tak things sindry right enough bit he's no so good at pittan them taegither again.*
thanadays: in those days: *Thanadays we hid ration books and yi couldna buy as many sweeties as yi wanted.*

<u>Exclamations</u>

aye aye: the most common greeting on meeting: *Aye, aye! No seen yi fur a while.*
bairns: especially in the form *Bairns! bairns!*, an exclamation of exasperation or surprise used by adults to adults.
beuy (fur that): an expression of surprise on hearing unexpected news.
bit-a-ting: a sentimental reference to, or about a baby or young child: *Hid's waakan noo the bit-a-ting.*
feenty bit: certainly not: *Feenty bit o me's gan tae wirk aal 'oors fur him.*
feenty thing: nothing at all: *Whit did I see? Feenty thing.*
fegs: indeed: *Fegs hid'll no be me thit helps him oot anywey.*
gad: an expression of disgust: also *gid-gad*: *Gad—I canna stand the smell o herreen boilan.*
lendy bit: certainly not: *Lendy bit o him'll ever change his weys.*
lokkars: goodness me!
min (fur that): an expression of surprise on hearing unexpected news.
na: no, frequently duplicated, *Na, na.*
nimm-nimms: good things to eat, used in talking to children.
niver spaek: a reply to a piece of upsetting news with which the listener is already acquaint: <u>Speaker</u>: *Did yi hear aboot Robbie last night?* <u>Listener</u>: *Niver spaek!*
stoop: 1. be quiet! 2. a reaction to an unbelievable piece of news.
wheesht: be quiet!

<u>Nouns</u>

air: a small quantity: *Pit a air o suggar in me tea.*
aizer: a fiercely burning domestic fire: *Whit a aizer o a fire yir pitten on!*
backend (the): harvest time.
bairn: child.
ben-end: rooms other than the living room in a house.
bere-bread: a bannock made from bere-meal, a form of barley (see *binnack* below).
binnack: a large flat scone, approximately 15 cms. across made from flour, bere meal or oat meal, milk and bicarbonate of soda.
bletherskate: someone who talks incessantly.
blide: happy: *Ah'm right blide thit yir been able tae come.*
blind-daa: a small dog fish.
bloody-sooker: horse fly.
blue-nild: mould on cheese.
bonie-words: prayers.
booick: a large pimple or boil.
boorwid tree: the elder tree.
brandie: stickleback.
bratto: a coarse apron, usually made from a sack.
breeks: trousers.

breer: sprouting corn.
brigstones/brigsteens: the pavement in front of a house.
bruck: 1. rubbish 2. nonsense.
buckie: a shell, the periwinkle.
buddum: bottom of a container, the sea etc.
burn: a stream.
but-end: the living room end of a house.
byre: cowshed.
char: infertile egg.
chingle: shingle.
claes: clothes.
clapshot: a traditional mixture of mashed potato and Swedish turnip.
clipe: 1. a smack: *When I wir peedie I got many a clipe fae the teachers.* 2. the leather strap formerly used by teachers to punish children.
cloot: rag, especially *dish cloot.*
cod: a pillow.
cog: 1. especially *bride's cog,* a wooden vessel filled with strong liquor passed among the wedding guests 2. the contents of a cog: *Ah'm niver taested such a grand cog.*
cookie: a light round bun made with yeast.
coolie: a knitted woollen hat.
cowe: only used in the sense *heather-cowe*, a single piece of heather pulled up by the root.
cubby: a large round container made of straw and with handles; it is used for holding wool, peat etc.
curly-doddie: clover head.
cut: humour: *He's in poor cut the day.*
differ: difference: *Hid disna mak any differ tae me.*
drowth: drying weather, especially in the phrase *tae mak a good drowth.*
eerie-orms: decorative carvings on furniture etc.
emmer-goose: red throated diver.
errans: shopping: *I must go and git twa-three errans.*
eum: excessive heat in a house in contrast to the temperature outside: *My whit a eum is in here.*
eun: a nasty smell eg. with an old wet rag.
face-washeen: telling off.
fleester: a light shower.
fleeter: 1. a torn piece of clothing 2. an extent of land etc.: *He his a fleeter o land on the brae teu.*
floory-bread: a bannock made from flour as opposed to bere-meal.
freck: an attention seeking child.
fuff: puff of wind.
gablo: crawling insect.
gaggle: sticky mess.

gansey: jersey.
gappus: fool.
geup: fool.
glap: 1. a sudden attack of illness 2. a chill, *Wrap ap weel in caes thoo gits a glap.*
gren: tiny bit, piece.
gravat: scarf.
green-nild: mould on cheese, bread.
grimleens: twilight.
guff: nasty smell.
gurr: 'sleep' in the eye.
gutter: mud.
haily buckie: hail stone.
hennie-hoose: chicken house.
ime: soot on bottom of pot.
hass: throat.
hookers: haunches.
horse-gokk: snipe.
hurl: a lift e.g. in a car or even a wheelbarrow!
iper: midden ooze.
jenny hunder legs: centipede.
kist: box.
kleg: a horsefly.
kringlos: heat shimmer.
lavro: lark.
lerblade: cormorant.
lintie: linnet.
longer: longing.
loom: red throated diver.
lug: ear.
lugget: a buffet on the ear.
lum: chimney.
lyre: the manx shearwater.
maggie hunder legs: centipede.
mallimak: fulmar petrel.
man-buddy: a man.
men folk: men.
Merry Dancers: aurora borealis.
messages: shopping
metteen: a grain of corn.
mither's bairn: spoilt child.
moss: a wet stretch of heather and moss covered land.
neb: 1. the beak of a bird 2. the nose (familiar).
neep: turnip.
netteen wire: wire netting.

nickum; a cheeky little child.
noust: boat shelter.
oat-bread: oat cake.
paddo: toad.
partan: crab.
peedie buddy: small person.
peedie finger: little finger.
peedie gren: a small quantity.
peedie meenit: short while.
peedie-breeks: jocular name for a child.
pelters: rags.
piltick: young coalfish.
pirls: 1. sheep dung 2. rabbit's droppings.
pit-by: something temporary.
plicko: a hand held torch.
plitter: a muddy mess.
pleenk: watery tea or beer.
puckle: a quantity: *Pit a puckle more cement in the mix min.*
puggy: stomach, especially of a child.
purm: cotton reel.
race: a short trip: *Ah'll come ower tae see yi a race the morn.*
raffle: confusion: *Whit a raffle me fisheen line's gin in.*
rain-goose: red throated diver.
red-ba: yolk of an egg.
reek: smoke.
ritto: black-headed gull.
roo: an untidy heap.
sark: shirt.
segs: reeds.
selkie: seal.
sharn: cow muck sticking to clothes, equipment etc.
sholt: pony.
side ditch: roadside ditch.
sillock: young coalfish.
skarfie: cormorant.
skootie-allan: Arctic skua.
skirlo: a small toy propeller carved from wood and spun in the wind.
skirp: a tear in clothing.
skitter: (vulgar) diarrhoea.
skootie: the starling.
skry: a teeming number: *Wir new neebors hiv an aafil skry o bairns.*
skurt: 1. the lap 2. the bottom of an apron held up and used as a carrying device: *Me granny used tae cairry paets in her skurt.*
slatero: woodlouse.

slerp: a rough coat (of paint): *Ah'm gae-an the boat a slerp o pent fur the winter.*
slygoose: shelduck.
sneck: door latch.
sneeshan: the coot.
sole-stockeens: stocking soles.
sook: drying weather: *Hid's makkan a grand sook the day.*
spaekalation: a topic of rumour.
spoot: razor fish.
steero: confusion: *Whit a steero the room wir in!*
stirleen: starling.
stoor: dust.
strip: stripe.
syes: chives.
syre: 1. the grating which covers a sewer 2. a sieve.
talders: rags.
tang: seaweed.
teebro: heat shimmer.
teeo: lapwing.
tirlo: a small toy propeller carved from wood and spun in the wind.
tirso: a weed, usually the 'dock'.
tishalago: coltsfoot.
took: a sip from a bottle.
trachle: difficult time: *Whit a trachle wir hin wi the silage the 'ear.*
trow: troll.
trowie-girse: fox-glove.
tuction: hard usage: *Yir no gan tae git anither bike efter the tuction the last wan got.*
tusker: tool for cutting peats.
twart-back: cross bearer in a roof.
tystie: black guillemot.
veet: a vet.
volo: field vole.
waal: well of water.
waddeen: wedding.
ware: seaweed.
wark: 1. work 2. difficulty: *Ah'm hin a wark wi me leg fae the ram doosed me.*
water-hen: moorhen.
water-pleep: snipe.
weet: rain: *Wir hin a ferfil o weet this last peedie while.*
weeks: corners of the mouth.
whassigo: excuse.
white-maa: seagull.
wife-buddy: a woman.
yackles: molar teeth.
yellow yarling: yellow hammer.

Verbs

andoo: to keep a boat in position by rowing gently against the tide.

bide: to stay.

birl: to spin around.

bogle: of a cow, to low or a child to cry loudly.

brett up: 1. to roll up e.g. the sleeves 2. to physically challenge someone bigger than oneself, *He bretted ap tae this man thit wis a piece bigger ur himsel.*

bulder: to rush precipitously.

cast up: to bring into conversation things that ought to be forgotten about.

chaest: to chase.

chap: 1. to knock on a door 2. to mash potatoes 3. to pinch (the finger etc.) by trapping it between two objects.

chapse: to eat noisily.

chilter: of liquid in a container, to swill around noisily.

clart/clert: to cover something thickly, usually with some objectionable substance e.g mud.

click: to snatch.

coup: to spill.

dilder: to shake, especially with cold.

doos: of a sheep or ram to butt.

dort: 1. of a bird, to abandon its nest 2. to pout.

eek oot: to economise by using sparingly: *We'll hae tae eek oot the butter till I git tae the shop.*

fa in tow wi: to associate with some disreputable person.

fend: of a hen or cat, to hunt for food.

flee: to fly: *The bird canna flee at aal.*

fleep: to turn inside out: *Fleep the pillow-caes first than hid's aisier tae pit in the pillow.*

flit: 1. to move house 2. to move a tethered animal.

gan: (rhymes with 'van') to stare vacantly.

gavse: to eat voraciously.

girn: of a child to make a moaning noise.

glab: to snatch.

glinder: to peer.

gock: to trick.

golder: to laugh loudly.

gulup: to gulp.

hint: to gather e.g. potatoes in the garden.

kittle: to tickle.

klank: of a hen to make a shrill cry, especially after laying.

kline: to spread e.g. butter: an old invitation to sit up to table was *Fa teu noo; brak and kline* i.e. Sit in now, break (your bread) and spread (it with butter).

lagger: to coat thickly and carelessly with some substance e.g. paint, tar etc.

lippen: to expect.

lowe: (rhymes with 'now') to burn with a flame.

madrom: anger.

magse: to walk with difficulty through mud etc.

mak weet: to rain.

mind: to remember: *I mind hid fine.*

mirr: of fingers etc., to tingle.

moor: of snow, to drift.

ower: to recover from an illness: *He's owered the 'flu noo and he's gan back tae his wark the morn.*

pleep: of an adult, to complain in a whining manner and unnecessarily about one's health, money etc. *She's aalwis pleepan aboot sometheen.*

poots: to sulk.

prog: to prick with a sharp object: *Mither—Kevin's jist proggèd me wi that dart.*

ramp: of a kettle etc to boil vigorously.

reek: 1. of a fire etc to smoke 2. to smell strongly.

rex: to stretch one's arms to reach something. *Rex in noo and help yirsel.*

rive: to tear.

share: to cut, especially peats.

sie: to strain e.g. potatoes or vegetables.

skail: to scatter: *Skail a puckle o the oats oot on the grund fur the hens.*

skeet: 1. to shoot water out of a narrow tube 2. of an object to slide quickly off a shiny surface 3. to skim a stone on the loch or on the sea.

skuther: to bruise the leg or arm and draw blood by coming in contact with a rough surface.

slock: to extinguish a candle, fire etc.

smook: of snow, to drift.

smoor: of snow, to drift.

sneeter: to laugh in an underhand way.

speer: to ask.

spret: 1. of a seam etc. to split 2. to jump out: *As soon as I opened the door the cat spret oot.*

spring: to strain a muscle: *Watch an no spring yirsel wi aal that lifting.*

stap: to cram: *Don't stap yir mooth so fill beuy—that's aafil bad manners.*

stoop: (vulgar) Shut up!

strick: to strike.

swee: 1. of a burn, injury etc., to smart 2. of crops on shallow soil, to wither.

think long: to long for: *Ah'm aalwis thinkan long fur home.*

think tae: to have an opinion of: *Whit are yi thinkan tae the new rules?*

tirl: to turn.

thraa: to twist: *I could niver mak mesel thraa the neck o a hen.*

thrapple: throat: *Pit this doon yir thrapple and yi'll feel better.*

tirl: to spin round.

tizz: of a child to cry affectedly.

trim: to repair.

trimse: to move around impatiently.

wap: to turn a cranking handle.

wip: to wrap: *If yi wip the string aroond hid, hid'll had hid a piece thighter.*

watch: to notice: *I watched that in The Orcadian.*

weengle: to twist round on a chair, especially to balance it on less than four legs!
  Stop weenglan on that owld chair beuy!

wheek: to snatch: *He wheekèd hid oot o me hand.*

yaggle: to cut roughly.

yarm: of a cat, to mew noisily.

yeuk: to itch.

Test your Fluency!

How well do you speak Orkney dialect? Try some of these!
Hoo weel dae yi spaek Orcadian? Try some o this wans.

1 He caught two trout in the loch today.
2 There were two women walking down the road; one woman was dressed in black.
3 It's a good distance to walk to the library these days.
4 Have you seen my toothbrush?
5 I've found five knives in the drawer.
6 I didn't have an exercise book with me.
7 I must get some shopping when I'm in town.
8 He has been working as a joiner in New Zealand.
9 What are you doing tomorrow morning?
10 He became ill tonight.
11 Just a little sugar please.
12 Many people have been to see how it works.
13 These are ours.
14 Everywhere one goes in Canada one meets Orkney people.
15 Then he surprised us by saying he had got a flight after all!
16 He often went to town on Mondays by bus.
17 The cow would not go in front of me so I had to go behind her.
18 I'm told that Magnus is very clever.
19 It's really good.
20 How do you do that?
21 There's a little bit left.
22 There's much to do before we've finished.
23 There aren't many people here tonight.
24 She lives in the house down the slope.
25 I took it from the cupboard.
26 Moreover, you have taken my clothes!
27 I haven't seen your sister since New Year (use the form based on English 'thou'.)
28 He didn't come anyway and so we went out. (don't use *anywey*).
29 So what can we do?
30 Mum—bring that through when you come.
31 I hear you are working at the newsagents.
32 What kind of work do you do?
33 There are men waiting here.
34 I'm sick of hearing that!

35 You are being really stupid.
36 I think one needs to take care today.
37 It's pouring with rain!
38 Why is that child crying its eyes out?
39 I shan't do that now.
40 I'm going to shop tomorrow.
41 Wouldn't I!
42 I heard she was going to have twins.
43 He found that he had it in his pocket after all!
44 He put it down then out he went.
45 I was going to go but I fell ill.
46 I have knitted two pairs of socks today.
47 He had hit him over the head.
48 You have taken a long time to get here. (use English 'thou' form)
49 I'm walking into town because I like walking.
50 You'll find difficulty parking there—there's parking behind the house.

For comment, e-mail your answers to gregor.lamb2@btinternet.com

References

Barry, G. *History of the Orkney Islands,* Edinburgh, 1808.

Flaws, M. and Lamb, G. *Orkney Dictionary*, Orkney Language and Culture Group, Orkney, 1996.

Lamb, G. *Orkney Wordbook*, Byrgisey, Orkney, 1995.

Robertson, T. A. and Graham, John J. *Grammar and Usage of the Shetland Dialect*, The Shetland Times, Lerwick, 1991.

Robinson, M. (Ed.) *The Concise Scots Dictionary*, Aberdeen University Press, 1985.

Thomson, A. J. and Martinet, A. V. *A Practical English Grammar*, Oxford University Press, 1986.

van Leyden, K. *Prosodic Characteristics of Orkney and Shetland Dialects,* University of Leyden, Holland, 2004.